# The Buyer's Guide to Affordable Antique Jewelry

### by Anna M. Miller

A Citadel Press Book
Published by Carol Publishing Group

*Cover. Top, Victorian gold earring set with pink topaz showing repoussé work along with design of scrolls and flowers. Bottom, green demantoid garnets, opals, make this turn-of-the-century crescent brooch especially desirable. (Courtesy Philip Stocker, F.G.A.)*

Copyright © 1993 Anna M. Miller

A Citadel Press Book
Published by Carol Publishing Group
Citadel Press is a registered trademark of Carol Communications, Inc.
Editorial Offices: 600 Madison Avenue, New York, N.Y. 10022
Sales and Distribution Offices: 120 Enterprise Avenue, Secaucus, N.J. 07094
In Canada: Canadian Manda Group, P.O. Box 920, Station U, Toronto,
    Ontario M8Z 5P9

Queries regarding rights and permissions should be addressed to Carol Publishing Group, 600 Madison Avenue, New York, N.Y. 10022

Carol Publishing Group books are available at special discounts for bulk
    purchases, for sales promotion, fund-raising, or educational purposes.
Special editions can be created to specifications. For details, contact:
Special Sales Department, Carol Publishing Group, 120 Enterprise Avenue,
    Secaucus, N.J. 07094

Manufactured in the United States of America

10  9  8  7  6  5  4  3  2  1

Library of Congress Cataloging-in-Publication Data

Miller, Anna M., 1933–
    The buyer's guide to affordable antique jewelry : how to find, buy, and care for fabulous antique jewelry / by Anna M. Miller.
        p.  cm.
    "Citadel Press Book."
    ISBN 0-8065-1411-6
    1. Jewelry—Collectors and collecting—United States. I. Title.
NK7312.M56  1993
739.27'075—dc20                                               92-37557
                                                                  CIP

# The Buyer's Guide to Affordable Antique Jewelry

*Dedication*

*To John, Eric,*
*Kay, and Bonnie,*
*with love*

## NOTE

The prices and values stated in *Buyer's Guide to Affordable Antique Jewelry* are actual figures obtained from retail antique jewelry dealers and estimated sales at auctions. Because the supply of and demand for antique jewelry varies, differences in prices from one geographical location to another may occur. The 1993 prices stated in this book, therefore, are to be viewed as guides, and not exact universal values.

# Contents

**PREFACE**                                                                IX

**ACKNOWLEDGMENTS**                                                         XII

**CHAPTER 1** Antique Jewelry: What You Need to Know  3
• *What Is Antique? Heirloom? Collectible? Period?*
• *Knowing Jewelry History Creates Added Interest* • *The
Importance of Circa Dating: Learning to Circa Date*
• *Georgian: 1714–1837* • *Victorian: 1837–1901* • *Art
Nouveau: 1880–1914* • *Arts and Crafts: 1890–1914*
• *Edwardian: 1901–1910* • *Art Deco: 1920–1940*
• *Retro: 1935–1950*

**CHAPTER 2** Lessons From the Professionals  30
•*Viewpoints and Tips From Collectors* • *Playing the Auction
Game* • *Buyer Beware* • *Avoid Mistakes*

**CHAPTER 3** The Wise Buyer  40
•*Learning the Language of Antique Jewelry* • *Gemstones*
• *The Most Basic Tool and How to Use It* • *Optional
Equipment* • *Is Your Jewelry Married?* • *How to Tell a
Reproduction* • *Learning to Judge Quality, Style, and
Workmanship* • *Repairs Affect Value*

**CHAPTER 4** What Is Affordable?  58
•*Bracelets* • *Brooches* • *Garnet Jewelry* • *Buttons Made Into
Jewelry* • *Chains* • *Crosses* • *Earrings* • *Lockets/Pendants*
• *Necklaces* • *Rings* • *Scarfpins and Stickpins* • *Watch Fobs*

• *What to Look for in Old Beads* • *Mourning Jewelry*
• *Military Sweetheart Badges* • *Propaganda Jewelry*

**CHAPTER 5** Collecting Cycles and Style Revivals          **105**
•*Trends, Fads, Fashions* • *Future Trends—The New
Antiques* • *Important Designer Names and Manufacturer's
Marks* • *How to Recognize Metals and Manufacturing
Methods* • *Metals* • *Hallmarks* • *More About Colored
Gemstones* • *Old Glass (Paste) Is Nice*

**CHAPTER 6** Where the Antique Jewelry Is Found          **124**
• *To Market, to Market* • *Stalking the Antique Jewelry Show*
• *What to Know Before Buying Antique Jewelry Overseas*
• *About the VAT Tax*

**CHAPTER 7** Dressing for the Hunt                        **136**
•*In the Eye of the Beholder* • *Too Many Cooks Spoil the
Broth* • *Lessons in Bargaining—It Never Hurts to Ask*
• *Asking the Right Questions—Getting the Right Answers*

**CHAPTER 8** Collecting by the Book                       **143**
•*How to Start a Collection* • *Building With a Plan*
• *Collecting a Single Item or Period* • *When and How to Get
Insurance* • *How to Get an Appraisal* • *Making a Personal
Inventory* • *Using Jewelry Price Guides*

**CHAPTER 9** Lost Treasures You Can Find!                 **151**
• *The Brunswick Diamond Feather Pin* • *The Brunswick
Blue Diamond* • *The Florentine Diamond* • *Emerald
Necklace-Pendant From the House of Savoy* • *The Rossetti
Pocket Watch* •*The Quedlinburg Treasure*

**CHAPTER 10** Caring for Your Antique Jewelry            **163**
•*Taking Care of Costume Jewelry* • *A Final Word*

**GLOSSARY** Antique and Period Jewelry Terms              **169**

**BIBLIOGRAPHY**                                            **175**

**INDEX**                                                   **177**

# $\mathcal{P}$REFACE

This guidebook is written out of my adoration for antique jewelry. While many people buy and wear contemporary jewelry, it takes a certain personality to be able to enjoy and develop a feeling for antique jewels. I hope to instill a desire for collecting and wearing antique jewelry by showing you why it is so special. In this book, we concentrate on today's most *affordable* treasures. These are the ones that were common in the past and can still be found and purchased today without causing serious financial wallet shock.

In the past few years, I have noted that while there is a plethora of books covering top-quality antique jewelry, including some on investing in jewelry, little advice can be found on the middle-market antique jewelry that we call "affordable." This guide attempts to address that void; to answer questions about antique jewelry, and offer caveats on collecting it.

Collecting, which historians believe comes from the age of the Victorians, requires more from you than just a casual interest. To be a true *collector*, you must also learn about historical background and develop an understanding of pricing structures and markets. Also, if you wish to have your antique jewelry reward you with price appreciation as well as personal satisfaction, you must arm yourself with product knowledge and information on cycles of styles. Not only does the accumulation of knowledge result in a wiser buyer, but also in a collector who will be positioned to discover treasures overlooked by peers, colleagues, and less-curious collectors. The reward is that nothing can match the excitement of making a *find* in the field of antique-jewelry collecting!

Since the early 1980s, I have taught classes and seminars about antique jewelry all over the United States and overseas. Classes are always filled with eager participants, including advanced collectors who want to hear more about the pleasures and pitfalls of buying and owning antique jewelry. Not all the interest stems from the desire to decorate their bodies: many collectors have become aware that such items are weathering inflation better than many other assets. Many also understand that owning a cache of antique jewelry affords the collector a concentration of wealth, as well as easy portability of that wealth.

I have not attempted to exhaustively cover any one aspect of this subject. Although the very best antique jewelry will certainly date from the eighteenth century and earlier (the days before mass production and machine-made), it is the jewels of the middle nineteenth century that are most often available to us today. Relatively few genuine jewels of the Georgian and earlier periods are in the marketplace. Most of the genuinely old items are either in museum or private collections. And, unfortunately after the French Revolution of 1793, fashion—including the jewelry—changed so dramatically that little remained in its original settings as stones were removed from their mountings and settings were melted down. Therefore, this book will primarily help you identify desirable nineteenth- and early-twentieth-century antique and heirloom jewelry.

For those with the inclination to start a collection but who may be procrastinating, wait no longer. Now is the time to build your collection while articles of jewelry are in good supply and are relatively inexpensive. Now is the time to identify your area of interest, research provenance, and discover the original uses of those fine old jewels.

A word about pricing: Change is an element of market economics and like any market you can expect jewelry prices to fluctuate depending upon fashion, supply and demand, geographical location and market level of sale. Although we attempted to keep a $1,500 maximum price for most jewelry, there are some items included that exceed our self-imposed limit. In most cases, we are simply compelled to point out value-making features or exceptional points of craftsmanship. At other times, however, we list the price of a piece of jewelry as what you are most likely to see in the normal jewelry antiques and auction marketplace, and we include it to extend the collector's knowledge of present-day pricing.

And here is one final thought for the collector: develop a passion for your subject. Because even if you have the disposable income for buying jewelry, a broad knowledge of the subject, and time to relentlessly pursue it, to be a successful and happy collector the one emotional ingredient you must possess is *passion* for the prize. Remember that the most beautiful jewelry—those pieces crafted with style, brilliant design, and finish—were overwhelmingly conceived by designer/craftsmen who were exhilarated by their art and craft. For, without a growing passion for antique jewelry to spur you on in your quest and excite your interest in its history and evolution, you may never achieve more than just a mediocre collection.

## ACKNOWLEDGMENTS

This book includes the ideas and suggestions offered by a number of friends, gemological colleagues, dealers, and collectors.

I would first like to acknowledge a special debt of gratitude to Joanna Angel for her editorial advice and expertise.

Then I wish to thank the following individuals for their generous help in both research and discussion of this subject, and for the valuable information they contributed: Lynette Proler; Bonnie Miller; Pam Abramson; David Atlas; Peggy Blackford; John Miller; Terry Blend; Charles Edwards; Steve Johnson; Kathy Kinev; Sandy Jones; Shirley Sue Swaab; Elaine and Ben Smith; Joel Bartsch, curator of Gems and Minerals Houston Museum of Natural Science; Herbert Duke, International Gem and Jewelry Shows, Inc.; Theresa Elley; Paula Hantman; C. G. Sloan & Company; Dr. John Grant; Ben Nobel, Jr.; Peggy Gottlieb; Dr. Joe Sataloff; Ellen J. Epstein; Vicki Eaton; Dr. William C. Metropolis, Harvard University; Pfarrer Friedemann GoBlau, Germany; Mary Jane Turner; Elizabeth Pierce Green; Paula Locklair, director and curator Old Salem; W. DiAnna Cannan, geologist and colleague in Indonesia; and Janet Zapata. Also, a special thanks to my business associate and mentor, Dr. Charles D. Peavy, for his encouragement as well as his wise critique.

I particularly wish to thank my colleagues in Great Britain for information that adds so much to this text; especially Philip Stocker, F.G.A., Registered Valuer for the National Association of Goldsmiths, for generously contributing information and photographs.

# The Buyer's Guide to Affordable Antique Jewelry

CHAPTER ONE

# Antique Jewelry: What You Need to Know

O nce when Mrs. John Jacob Astor, doyenne of society's Four Hundred, was questioned about the suitability of wearing diamonds during the daytime. her cool reply was reported to be, "Only if you have them, dear."

Today, buyers and collectors of antique jewels might be tempted to give the same response to those who question the suitability of wearing antique jewelry with modern clothing. The devotees of this fashion combination are fond of pointing out that the juxtaposition of antique jewelry and contemporary clothing underscores the good taste and style sense of the individual.

Only a few decades ago, antique jewelry, if found at antique shows at all, was relegated to a single showcase of one or two dealers. Only in the last few years has antique, estate, and vintage jewelry been available in increasing supply, as the demand for it has soared across the country.

What is so special about the old pieces? Basically, finding

and collecting it gives many a feeling of continuity and family. Even if the antique brooch or ring has not been passed down in your own family, it still carries the same sentimental appeal because it has been worn and cherished. Also, many upwardly mobile business people and professionals are discovering that wearing antique jewelry helps promote their style and image, says something about them as individuals, and reveals how they define themselves.

Dealers have begun to realize that antique jewelry represents good value, provides instant gratification to the purchaser, and is being viewed as an art form contributing to our cultural history as much as antique furniture and decorative art. Indeed, many pieces of antique jewelry are strong conversation pieces with a fascinating history or origin of their own.

Another strong argument for collecting antique jewelry is that today's machine-produced items are frequently of questionable quality while most (but not all) antique jewelry offers design, style, and craftsmanship. Also, often it is the value of an item that first arouses interest, and the notion that collecting antique jewelry seems to offer a faster payoff of appreciable assets than many other types of antiques. There is, however, one element that stands above all others as the most compelling support for antique jewelry: it is the last bastion of *affordable* collecting. Available from less than $100 to thousands of dollars, antique jewelry is still underpriced compared to many other antiques such as Old Master paintings, silver, and objets d'art.

Although affordability is a relative term, in this guide "affordable" describes antique jewelry priced from a few dollars up to $1,500 in the current retail market. Within this price range are thousands of desirable and collectible jewelry items with appeal to men and women. The key to their detection lies in learning about what they are, their design, and their place in jewelry history.

# WHAT IS ANTIQUE? HEIRLOOM?
# COLLECTIBLE? PERIOD?

Many people believe that anything old is an antique. Some think that if it belonged to their grandmother, for instance, it is automatically considered an antique. However, there are standards by which the word "antique" is defined and belonging to grandmother is not one of them. According to the United States Customs Bureau, antique jewelry is any jewelry one hundred or more years old. Thus the base for antique jewelry grows yearly.

One reason people buy antique jewelry is that they like the idea of buying a bit of history. It makes an old piece more attractive if you know, for instance, that light-colored gemstones became more popular than darker ones after 1900 because under the new electric lights, dark colors looked more garish.

*Heirloom*—sometimes called "estate" or "vintage" jewelry, is "previously owned" jewelry. It may or may not have been passed from one generation to another in the same family and can vary in age from a few decades to 100 years old. The term "estate" does not necessarily mean that the previous owners are dead. In its broadest sense, "estate" encompasses everything from centuries-old jewelry to the collectibles of the 1990s. The sellers of "antique" jewelry often take liberties with the terms "estate" or "vintage" and use them synonymously. Most often, they are simply trying to point up the intrinsic value of the piece; the value of the precious metals or gemstones.

*Collectibles* are jewelry items gathered from any period in time or from any jewelry designer or manufacturer (often contemporary) where the piece is *usually* no longer in production. The individual purchases and collects according to his or her desire or interests, and a collection may span several periods, designers or categories of design.

*Period* jewelry is jewelry that is defined by a framework of a specific time and style. The periods have been arranged chronologically for easier recognition and understanding of the style of particular eras:

**Georgian: 1714–1837**
**Early Victorian: 1837–1860**
**Mid-Victorian: 1860–1880**
**Late Victorian: 1880–1901**
**Art Nouveau: 1880–1914**
**Arts and Crafts: 1890–1914**
**Edwardian: 1901–1910**
**Art Deco: 1920–1940**
**Retro: 1935–1950**

The jewelry items made before the eighteenth century are very scarce and, if found, are often expensive and do not fit into our criteria for "affordable" jewelry. Roman (c. A.D. 100–300) and Sassanian (Persian c. A.D. 600–700) intaglio rings are usually available through auction and dealers for $500-$1,000. If the intaglios have been reset in Victorian settings, they can go for as little as $300-$500. Roman earrings (c. A.D. 100–300) in gold can also be found frequently for $500-$1,000. The greatest production of jewelry occurred in the mid-1800s when jewelry began to be mass-manufactured. It is from this period and onward that the greatest number of affordable jewelry pieces can be found. Locating antique jewels comes down to a matter of logistics: the more distant the period, the fewer pieces are available in the open market.

# KNOWING JEWELRY
## HISTORY CREATES
## ADDED INTEREST

Jewelry design has always been influenced by the cultural and economic development in the country of its origin, by the available materials, and by the individual talents of the artists of the time. Customs, geography, religion, and laws have determined who could wear what type of jewelry. War, peace, cultural revivals, expositions, explorations, and inventions have all affected jewelry design. However, nothing has influenced the popularity of jewelry more than fashion, and since the late eighteenth century it has been fashion that has dominated the wearing of jewelry and its style. The appetite for jewelry among the masses exploded when wearing jewelry became no longer the exclusive domain of royalty and the nobility in the wake of political and social upheavals in Europe. Furthermore, the Industrial Revolution and the resulting birth of mass production made jewelry more affordable, and wearing it became a proclamation by the middle class of its new rights ensuing from its new socioeconomic importance.

All of the aforementioned periods developed their own unique styles and designs, resulting in a wide variety of antique jewelry. While there are still bargains to be found, you must know what you are seeing when you see it. Most of us tend to regard the products of the past in a nostalgic and uncritical way, believing that anything antique must be beautiful and well crafted. Nothing could be farther from the truth. From the middle-1800s, when the middle class became an important buying group, much of the mass-produced jewelry was shoddily made. Invariably, the best pieces were impossible to reproduce by machine. While the most prolific years for jewelry production were from 1830 to 1930 and some items were well done, most were mediocre, and some were quite poor.

## THE IMPORTANCE OF CIRCA DATING: LEARNING TO CIRCA DATE

In separating periods and styles of jewelry, you should know how to circa date. Circa dating is the establishment of a date of origin for the piece of jewelry. However, "circa" just approximates a date; it covers a ten-year window on either side of the given date. A circa date of 1820 indicates a date somewhere from 1810 to 1830.

Circa dating is vital to correct identification, and ultimately to value. A good beginning for learning how to circa date is studying the elements of design (motifs) and style that play a key role in the jewelry of a particular period. There are fewer styles than dates that should be kept in mind, and some designs and motifs were more popular in one period than another. Also, some gemstones and metals were used more extensively—sometimes exclusively—in various periods.

However, there is a caveat. It is true that various motifs are clues to age simply because they were used more widely during certain times, but there can be no dogmatic dating of pieces just because of a particular design. Historically, jewelry fashion periods have overlapped in Europe and the United States. When a style was peaking in North America, it was waning in Europe. And some designs, like flowers, have been popular motifs in jewelry since early Greek times. The rose was the motif of the island of Rhodes, used since c. 500 B.C.

Learning to circa date takes practice and patience. Many

jewelers do not have a clue to the identification of some of the items they are selling, let alone the ability to circa date them. For example, a jeweler recently prepared an appraisal for a customer describing a lapis lazuli antique scarab (the most precious and sacred symbol of eternal life of the ancient Egyptians) as a "small rodentlike creature." Actually, there are specific dating methods for scarabs. Some are worth huge sums of money!

## GEORGIAN
## 1714–1837

The Georgian period is usually thought of as that time covering the reigns of England's King George I through George IV. In this era, jewelry was made almost entirely by hand and is distinguished by its excellent craftsmanship. Beauty was created in all forms by artists, architects, cabinetmakers, and jewelers.

The Georgian period covered the time of gemstone faceting and the development of faceted gemstones. Diamonds are especially characteristic of this era. Much of the glittering diamond jewelry was the direct result of advanced cutting techniques and the final emergence of the round brilliant cut with its fifty-eight facets in the early eighteenth century. The table-cut diamond preceded the rose-cut, which was developed about 1520. Both styles can still be found in antique jewelry.

Silver settings were commonly used to intensify the whiteness and brightness of the diamonds. And the silver-topped 18-karat yellow gold mountings are often clues to circa dating jewelry from this era. In addition, both diamonds and colored gemstones were set with tin-foiled backs in

**Fig. 1–1** *A Georgian parure in 18-karat yellow gold with turquoise, in its original fitted box. The parure consists of a diadem, brooch, earrings, and pair of brooches which can be joined as a necklace. (Courtesy Philip Stocker, F.G.A.)*

closed settings to heighten the radiance of the gems and dramatize their color.

The most popular gemstones in Georgian jewelry were diamonds, pink topaz—especially Russian pink topaz—blue sapphires, emerald, dark red garnets, and paste (glass).

Paste became very popular in England, France, and Spain during the eighteenth century. The public's demand for cheap jewelry, along with the prevalence of highwaymen, created a market for paste jewelry. It is interesting that using the word *paste* for glass was derived from the Italian word *pasta*. The early Venetian glassmakers poured molten glass and worked it while it had the consistency of spaghetti.

Both men and women wore an abundance of jewelry during the Georgian era. It was common for men to wear jeweled buttons on their coats and the knees of their breeches, and pocket watches with a variety of watch fobs. Fashionable men wore jeweled buckles on their shoes.

Women favored either a full jewelry parure with a number of matching pieces (necklace, ring, brooch, earrings, and bracelet); or demi-parure with only two or three matching pieces. Their value may double if the jewelry is found in its original fitted box (Fig. 1–1).

A distinctive jewelry item was the aigrette, a hair or

Fig. 1–2 *(left) An aigrette (entremblant) brooch or hair ornament had stiff wires mounted with gems that moved with the wearer. An elaborate version of the girandole earring; the style had many variations. (Courtesy Dover Publishing Company)*

Fig. 1–3 *(above) A cut-steel butterfly brooch typical of its period can still be found priced about $100. (Photo by Peggy Blackford)*

brooch ornament set on springs that trembled when the wearer walked or moved her head. This phenomenon was called *en tremblant.* The Sévigné (bow) brooch was also popular, and girandole earrings, a style featuring three dangling pearls or gems from a boat-shaped or horizontal bar were fashionable (Fig. 1–2).

Cut-steel, like the mineral marcasite, was initially substituted for diamonds for those who could not afford the genuine article. Marcasite and cut-steel jewelry were the Georgian equivalent of costume jewelry.

In the late eighteenth century bits of steel were cut and faceted (Fig. 1–3), in a six-faced pyramid with flat backs and then individually riveted into place on a mounting. This technique, used from 1770 to 1840, is one way to identify early cut-steel work. After 1840, the faceted bits were riveted onto plates, sheets, or strips of metal.

# GEORGIAN-AT-A-GLANCE

## Motifs Most Frequently Found in Georgian Jewelry

• The Sévigné bow—A softly draped, somewhat floppy looking bow • hearts • floral garlands • ribbons • stars

**Fig. 1–4**
*Cannetille is an arrangement of wires that forms a filigree pattern. The work was popular in England in the early nineteenth century. Gold cannetille articles are usually handmade, silver ones are often stamped out. (Courtesy Elizabeth Pierce Green.)*

## Designs and Styles in Jewelry

• Openwork gold filigree designs • Cannetille, (Fig. 1–4) a tightly wound gold wirework
• Repoussé ("pushed back": designs in relief created by hammering from the back)
• Closed-back mountings • Long, hollow gold chains • Finely handcarved hardstone cameos
• Square-shaped brooches with pearl borders
• Aigrettes • Girandole earrings
• Ring with crowned-heart motif • Enamel or engraving ornamentation

## Gemstones and Metals Used

• Pinchbeck (an alloy of copper and zinc) • 18-Karat yellow gold • silver • diamond
• emerald • ruby • topaz • sapphire • garnet • turquoise • pearl • coral • marcasite (iron pyrite)
• cut-steel • paste (glass) • foil-back glass and foil-back natural gems

## Historical Footnote

The Georgian era was an age of opulence and self-indulgence in beauty and luxury by royalty, aristocracy, and a wealthy merchant class. Catherine the Great's 1762 coronation must have been one of the most overwhelming sights of the day. It was recorded that her royal robe was 75 yards long, and it took 55 men to carry it as she walked. There were lace ruffles on the sleeves, pearl and diamond buttons on her gown. She wore an ermine cape over her shoulders. Atop her head Catherine wore a crown with 2,564 diamonds and pearls, along with one gigantic and perfect ruby.

# VICTORIAN:
## 1837–1901

Queen Victoria of England reigned from 1837 to 1901. Her monarchy is the longest in British history. Jewelry historians have divided her reign into three periods for easier examination of the designs and motifs of the jewelry: Early Victorian, Mid-Victorian and Late Victorian. Each of these periods lasted approximately twenty years. Because Victoria loved jewelry and wore and promoted its use among her subjects, Great Britain became a major jewelry-making center. In fact, during the Victorian age, ladies of all means considered themselves undressed if their fashion accessories did not include earrings,

**Fig 1-5** *A collection of jewelry from the Victorian period that is both affordable and in good supply. Pictured from top clockwise: A Victorian 18K yellow gold ruby and bloodstone bracelet $1,500–$2,000; yellow gold, pearl, and cameo pendant brooch with tassel $300–$500; yellow gold and sardonyx cameo ring $700–$900; yellow gold and turquoise cabochon dangle earrings $700–$900; and a bracelet composed of eleven Victorian slides (originally used on watch chains). The slides are set with an assortment of gemstones, and the bracelet is completed with a Victorian snake-head clasp $2,000–$2,500. (Courtesy C. G. Sloan & Co. Auctioneers. © Peter Harholdt Studio.)*

brooches, necklaces, rings, chatelaines (long chains with dangling implements), bracelets, hair ornaments, and long chains to wear on muffs, watches and eyeglasses (Fig. 1–5).

The majority of the jewelry we collect today was produced in this period, sustained and driven by the new technologies like the pin-making machine. The machine, created in 1832, allowed numerous ways to attach ornaments to both hair and garments. By the mid-1800s, jewelry was being manufactured with a variety of precious metals and gemstones, as well as in cheaper metals with semi-precious gemstones. Gold was plentiful due to its discovery in both American and Australia. The electroplating process for coating base metal with silver or gold developed a look-alike precious metal substitute, which was eagerly accepted by the buying public.

In England precious gold jewelry was manufactured in 18-karat gold until 1854 when 9-, 12-, and 15-karat gold was introduced and legalized in order to meet foreign jewelry competition. Although some of the jewelry from that era is marked, the British government did not require jewelers to mark their goods during the nineteenth century; consequently, there is a characteristic lack of makers' marks (manufacturers marks) or hallmarks (which set forth the date and quality grade of the piece) on the metal settings.

Upon the death of her consort, Prince Albert, in 1861, Queen Victoria proclaimed an extended period of mourning; this set the mode of using black jet, onyx, and human hair in jewelry. Thousands of clasped hands in jet and onyx, crosses in onyx, often with pearls (signifying tears) used as border, and motifs of doves and garlands can be found from this period. When, after one year, half-mourning was permissible, the colors of gems used in this jewelry turned to grayish, mauve, or purple stones.

Collecting mourning jewelry offers great possibilities because of the large quantities available, affordable, and

## VICTORIAN-AT-A-GLANCE

### Motifs Most Frequently Found In Victorian Jewelry

•Bows • serpents • doves • hearts • crowns • crosses • angels • monograms • feathers • knots • arabesques • hands • grapes • quatrefoils • thistle • wheat • garlands • stars • arches • arrows • crescent moons • ribbons • Celtic images • eyes • scrollwork • tassels

### Designs and Styles in Jewelry

•"Regard" and "Posy" rings •Hair jewelry • Souvenir jewelry • Archaeological jewelry • Etruscan Revival designs • Egyptian Revival designs • Algerian knot designs

### Gemstones and Metals Used

• Silver (popular for daytime wear) • pinchbeck • multicolor gold from 9 to 22 karats fineness • gold gilt (electro-gilt used in 1844, after that mercury-gilding) • diamond • onyx • glass • cameos • carnelian • amber • coral • garnet • enamel • emerald • opal • pearl • peridot • ruby • sapphire • seed •pearl • topaz • turquoise • bog oak • ivory • jet • micromosaic • lava • marcosite • cut steel • tortoise shell • human hair

### Historical Footnote

Queen Victoria tried to promote English fashion, arts, and jewelry. When the public's penchant for opal jewelry was stifled by a Sir Walter Scott novel which spoke of the opal as an unlucky stone, Victoria attempted to revive its popularity by giving opal jewelry to her friends and family when she attained the throne.

It has been rumored that the French government, taking their cue from Scott, paid some gossipmongers to spread the idea that wearing opals was bad luck if they were not one's birthstone, hoping to destroy England's hold on the opal business.

English jewelers had a particular advantage in marketing this gemstone because of the discovery of great opal mines in Australia

The turquoise was a particular favorite of Victoria's, and she gave turquoise rings to each of her ladies-in-waiting upon her marriage to Albert. The rings were designed with a hand-painted portrait of Victoria set in a border of turqoise cabochons.

presently being overlooked. You can amass a good collecion
in a short time if you do not find this jewelry strange or mor-
bid.

Cameos are another item popular during the Victorian
era; Queen Victoria was especially fond of shell cameos.
During her reign, the classic subjects traditionally carved on
cameos changed from scenes of mythology and legend to the
sentimental motif with an anonymous female profile.
Although Queen Victoria is credited with increasing the popularity of the snake motif, the design has been used throughout jewelry history.

Ornamental motifs on jewelry centered strongly on the
Greek key, grapes, vines, leaves, hands, serpents, hearts, flowers, and crescent moons. Popular gemstones included
amethyst, opal, garnet, peridot, coral, citrine, turquoise, and
aquamarine. Gutta percha (a rubber material discovered in
1840 and used in mourning jewelry), bog oak, human hair,
tortoise and ivory were also used. Because of excavation in
Pompeii and Nineveh, archaeological designs were of interest
to the public. Tiger-claw jewelry was en vogue because of the
British empire in India. The cabochon cut in garnets, moonstones, opals and amber was popular. Romance and senti-
mentality were major themes of the Victorian age.

## ART NOUVEAU
## 1880–1914

Art Nouveau began as an innovation of design in both the
fine arts and architecture in the late nineteenth century and
lasted until World War I. At the turn of the century, there
were advances in science and technology and an expansion in
art and architecture. The Industrial Revolution created a back-

lash of artistic revolt that cul-
minated in a new form of
expression that came to be
known as Art Nouveau.

The jewelry motifs from
this era generally follow three
schools of design: new art,
crafts, and traditional. The old
Greek and Roman motifs were
combined with medieval
European images, iconogra-
phy from the romantic
Victorian period (Fig. 1–6),
and design concepts from the
Orient.

**Fig. 1–6** *Characteristic of the Art
Nouveau period jewelry is this
plique-à-jour enameled, silver, and
colored-gemstone dragonfly
brooch. Blue and green plique-à-
jour enameled wings and tail are
accentuated with white translucent
enamel. The piece is further decorated with green and red gemstones $700–$900. (Courtesy
C. G. Sloan & Co. Auctioneers.
©Peter Harholdt Studio.)*

Among the motifs found
in Art Nouveau jewelry, the
most characteristic is the sinu-
ous and curvilinear line; nude
or seminude female figures;
and female heads with long,
flowing hair posturing in a
languorous attitude. Whiplash
curves, sunbursts, crescents,
and a bizarre combination of female figures, insects, and
plants were combined in designs with a dreamlike quality.
The jewelry has an eroticism typical of Art Nouveau design.

French Art Nouveau jewelry typifies the most exciting
and beautiful work. The finest French Art Nouveau jewelry
was produced in 18-karat gold and utilized innovative sculp-
tured effects, quality workmanship, and unsurpassed enameling technique. Many French jewelers worked in the Art
Nouveau style, but the one most widely recognized for his
designs and artistry was René Lalique. He combined both

inexpensive materials like ivory, and horn (it has been reported that he often visited stockyards to purchase it) with expensive gems.

Art Nouveau jewelry was also being made in America by such well-known companies as Tiffany, Marcus & Company, and Kohn & Krementz. The jewelry was commonly made in 10-, 14-, or 18-karat yellow gold. Many jewelers of the period stamped their names or marks on their jewelry. American jewelers also mass-produced silver jewelry in the Art Nouveau style. Mass production contributed to a decline in the quality of the jewelry, and ultimately to the desirability of the Art Nouveau jewelry.

The jewelry of the Art Nouveau period stressed artistry and enameling with colored gemstones used to dramatize a design. Diamonds, sapphires, rubies and emeralds were used mostly as accents, in contrast to earlier periods, when gemstones were principal design elements. When colored gems were used, their color was the most important element, and soft and subtle shades were emphasized. Most favored were moonstones, opals, chalcedony, peridot, amethyst, aquamarine, topaz, mother-of-pearl, lapis lazuli, rock crystal, and turquoise. The cabochon cut was preferred. Jewelry from this era will frequently be set with synthetic rubies because scientists were succeeding in producing synthetic gemstones. In 1885 Auguste Victor Louis Vernéuil created synthetic rubies. Imitation emeralds, called *soudé* (French for soldered) were often used by jewelry designers. They were constructed of two layers of rock crystal with a green gelatinous layer cemented between them. To the unwary, the effect is startlingly emeraldlike.

# ART NOUVEAU-AT-A-GLANCE

## Motifs Most Frequently Found in Art Nouveau Jewelry

• Whiplash curves • human forms with insect wings • asymmetry • women with flowing hair • romanticism• butterflies • dragonflies • peacocks • grasshoppers • bees • wasps • swans • owls • bats • flowers • snakes

## Designs and Styles in Jewelry

• The "Lalique" style of jewelry in gold, pearls and brilliantly colored translucent enamel • Revival of the "sculptural" jewelry of the High Renaissance centuries depicting animals and human figures in gold, pearls, gemstones, and enamel • Japanese art themes in nature design • Repoussé widely used

## Gemstones and Metals Used

Ivory • horn • enamel • synthetic ruby and sapphire • quartz crystal • moonstone • lapis lazuli • carnelian • demantoid garnet • malachite • mother-of-pearl • opal • diamond • gold • silver • gold-filled • gold-plated • copper • steel • marcasite • vulcanite

## Historical Footnote

Queen Lydia Liliuokalani was the last queen of Hawaii (1891–1893); she died in 1917. In 1909 she decided to sell her crown jewels to found an orphanage in her name. Among the collection were hundreds of diamonds, including a 42-carat canary-yellow diamond, a gift to Queen Liliuokalani from Queen Victoria during Victoria's Royal Jubilee in 1887.

The diamond was presented to the queen in a 22-karat yellow-gold box with the initials of Queen Victoria set on top of the box along with the name of Queen Liliuokalani in her native language, with the date the gift was given: 1885. Gold figures on the sides of the box told the story of Hawaii.

The canary-yellow diamond has now been lost forever. In 1992, inquiries were made into its whereabouts, and it was discovered that the diamond had been sent to a cutter in Belgium and recut.

The present size or whereabouts of the diamond is unknown. The whereabouts of the precious 22-karat gold presentation box is also unknown.

# ARTS AND CRAFTS
# 1890–1914

The Arts and Crafts movement coexisted with Art Nouveau and highlighted the *aesthetic* rather than the *monetary* value of the materials. Englishman Charles Robert Ashbee pioneered the movement and tried to educate the public to appreciate Pre-Raphaelite (romantic) styles in design while promoting understanding of the importance of fine craftsmanship.

## ARTS AND CRAFTS-AT-A-GLANCE

### Motifs Most Frequently Found
### in Arts and Crafts Jewelry

- Designs of nature: flowers, leaves, garlands
- abstract designs

### Designs and Styles in Jewelry

- Brooches in peacock motif
- Rings and pendants in abstracts

### Gemstones and Metals Used

- Silver is the most popular metal
- base metals • amber • horn • ivory • blister pearls • cabochon-cut garnet • amethyst • moonstone • turquoise • enamel

### Noted Craftsmen

- Charles R. Ashbee • Arthur Gaskin • Jessie King
- Arthur Liberty—creator of the "Liberty Style"
- Henry Wilson

Ashbee disliked commercially produced jewelry and believed that the monetary value of jewelry should not be important to either craftsman or buyer. He wanted artisans to totally reject commercially mass-produced jewelry and concentrate on handmade jewelry which used inexpensive materials. Precious gold was touted as a contemptible metal because of its symbol of personal wealth; Art and Crafts artisans substituted silver and base metals. Designs are generally abstract or feature naturalistic themes like flowers. Use of enamels and cabochon-cut gemstones instead of faceted ones is typical of Arts and Crafts.

Handmade, however, does not necessarily mean well made, and today's collector is cautioned that some of the poorest-crafted jewelry will be found among articles from this time. It is worth noting that a great deal of the shoddy work can be attributed to students or jewelry amateur craftsmen.

# EDWARDIAN
# 1901–1910

The Edwardian period identifies the jewelry crafted between the Victorian and Art Nouveau periods, when Edward VII sat upon the throne of England. He arrived as monarch late in his life, and had already established an ostentatious court style. His reign was a continuation of the lavish display of wealth. Edward married Alexandra of Denmark, and their fondness for wearing and displaying jewelry had a profound influence on the style of this era. Jewelry collectors who like to gather items from the Edwardian era are soon aware that the jewelry overall is of excellent quality in materials and workmanship. The heavy use of diamonds and platinum are chief characteristics of Edwardian jewelry. Although platinum was known ear-

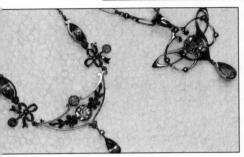

**Fig. 1–7** (top)Platinum and diamonds characterize jewelry from the Edwardian period, as well as the setting techniques of the knife-edge and millegraining. Millegraining is a raised-and-beaded edge on the settings. They can be found priced about $500 and up.

**Fig. 1–8** (right) This Edwardian platinum, diamond, and sapphire pendant necklace is especially desirable because it is offered with its original presentation box. This lovely piece exhibits both knife-edge and millegrained settings. (Courtesy Philip Stocker, F.G.A.)

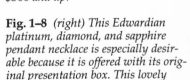

**Fig. 1–9** (left)The lavaliere, a delicately designed pendant necklace worn in the period between 1890 and 1910 spans both the Late Victorian and Edwardian eras and can be referred to as a transitional type of jewelry. Both of these lavalieres are set with demantoid garnets, a favorite gemstone of Edward. Priced about $1,000–$1,500. (Courtesy Philip Stocker, F.G.A.)

lier, it took the development of a torch hot enough to work the metal comfortably (about 1890), before its use was commonplace. Platinum combined with the new gemstone-cutting techniques and setting styles created designs of delicacy and elegance. A setting called the *knife-edge* (Fig. 1–7) resulted in an almost-invisible mounting where the gemstone seemed to float without support. *Millegrained* (raised edges) settings made diamonds appear larger, especially when set in platinum. When the trend for platinum settings declined in about 1910, white gold took its place as the metal of choice for diamonds.

## EDWARDIAN-AT-A-GLANCE

### Motifs Most Frequently Found in Edwardian Jewelry

• Good-luck symbols • horseshoes • wishbones • doves • hearts • acanthus leaves • laurel wreaths • ribbon bows • flowers • flower garlands • fish • peacocks • ducks • foxes • jumping horses • horsemen with carriages • bows and arrows • sun • stars • moon

### Designs and Styles of Jewelry

• Diamond hair ornaments • Dog collars (multistrand choker necklace. These were popular because Alexandra always wore them to hide a surgical scar on her throat) • Collet (bezel)-set stones • Pierced metal mountings • Handkerchief style pendants • Negligée pendants • Bar brooches • Filigreed platinum pendants with knife-edge and millegrain settings • Long bead or pearl sautoirs with and without tassel ends • Drop earrings

### Gemstones and Metals Used

Pearl • diamond • amethyst • peridot • demantoid garnet • ruby • sapphire • emerald • opal • platinum • silver • white gold (after 1910)

Distinctive to the Edwardian period and currently affordable are pearl sautoirs with tassels, pearl dog collars, negligée pendants, bar brooches, and bangle bracelets (Figs. 1–8, 1–9).

## ART DECO
## 1920-1940

When the serpentine lines, sensuous curves, and botanical motifs of Art Nouveau began to bore the public, Art Deco design jarred them right into the Jazz Age. Art Deco was a style revolution of straight, clean lines and angles over curves and fluid lines, bold colors over muted ones.

Art Deco drew life and inspiration from several sources: the introduction of cubism into the art world; the Russian ballet, which moved to Paris after the Bolshevik Revolution, because of its colorful costuming; Asian, Islamic, Indian, African and Egyptian art; the women's suffrage movement; and the Machine Age, exemplified by the automobile. It was a societal time of freedom of expression as women began to exert their independence, first discovered during World War I. Smoking was en vogue and women (no longer subject to arrest for smoking in public) took up the habit with gusto. This, of course, launched a line of fine smoking accessories, many bejeweled, designed and promoted by celebrated jewelry makers. This is all collectible memorabilia today. New styles of earrings were needed to fill the need created when the short bobbed hairstyle suddenly exposed women's ears, and because women had ceased to pierce their ears years earlier. The screw-back earring (1901–1910) was immensely popular. The sacklike chemise dress, which eliminated the need for constricting corsets, was ornamented by long ropes of beads or pearls.

## ART DECO-AT-A-GLANCE

### Motifs Most Frequently Found in Art Deco Jewelry

•Cubism • geometric • floral • abstract
Oriental • Aztec • Egyptian • Islamic • Russian
• architectural

### Designs and Styles of Art Deco Jewelry

• "Fruit salad" look popular • Dress clips are uniquely
Art Deco • Cocktail watch

### Gemstones and Metals of the Art Deco Period

Diamond • ruby • emerald • sapphire • rock crystal
• carnelian • onyx • chrysoprase • marcasite • jade
• ivory • lapis lazuli • coral • jet • Bakelite • turquoise
• mother-of-pearl • glass • synthetic gemstones: ruby, sapphire,
emerald • platinum • white gold
• silver •tricolor gold

### Historical Footnote

Gabrielle Chanel made costume jewelry acceptable and fashionable by launching a trend for using colored-glass jewelry and imitation pearls in the 1920s.

Typical of the Art Deco era is jewelry with a "fruit salad" look; rings and brooches made with a combination of diamonds, carved rubies, carved emeralds, and carved sapphires. Platinum, white gold and tricolor—yellow, rose, and green—gold held their places as favorite precious metals. One of the most popular articles of jewelry during the 1930s was the diamond straightline bracelet. In the 1980s this style was

**Fig. 1–10** *The cocktail watch debuted during the Art Deco period. Collectors seek unusual watches, like this Art Deco mixed metal and glass pendant watch, left, on a flexible link and bar chain. The watch back is decorated with engraved circular disk depicting a woman with a dog. Estimated price $400–$500. The 14K white gold and diamond lady's Hamilton wristwatch can be found priced about $300–$500. The white gold, diamond, and sapphire straightline bracelet was renamed the "tennis" bracelet in the 1980s. This style estimated $800–$1,000. (Courtesy C. G. Sloan & Co. Auctioneers. ©Peter Harholdt Studio.)*

revived as the tennis bracelet which, because of its simple but elegant design, remains trendy and collectible today.

One purely Art Deco material is a substance called Bakelite, an early plastic invented by Dr. Leo Baekeland in 1909, while he was searching for a rubber substitute to use in electrical insulation. Jewelry designers were excited about Bakelite because it could be molded so easily and colored so dramatically. Glitzy Bakelite bracelets, pins, earrings, necklaces, and pendants in geometric, fruit, and floral designs are available today in secondhand jewelry markets. Because the Bakelite pieces were typical of middle-class jewelry during the 1900s, they are among the most affordably collectible items from the Art Deco period today.

Some of the familiar motifs associated with the Art Deco era are both Egyptian and Oriental. There have been several Egyptian jewelry revivals and, with Howard Carter's discovery of Tutankhamen's tomb in 1923, the demand for archaeological reproductions was renewed. The Oriental influence was strong in Art Deco jewelry because of new trade agreements between the United States and Japan. The Asian influence manifested itself in jewelry designed with both carved and smoothly polished jade and coral in pendants, bracelets, earrings, and objets d'art. The lattice motif, along with the pagoda, dragons, Fu dogs, fish, and disks were popular carved motifs.

Making its debut in the Art Deco era was the cocktail wristwatch. This timekeeping accessory gained immediate and universal appeal among the gilded youth of the Jazz Age (Fig. 1–10).

# RETRO
# 1935-1950

During the Retro period, American-made jewelry began to acquire its own special style. This was an era when the United States was emerging from the Great Depression, war was raging in Europe, and France was no longer the jewelry-design center of the world. The influence of the crowned heads and nobility of Europe and the fads created by the aristocracy were no longer viable in a changing world. World War II closed the royalty-led chapter of jewelry history and replaced it with trend-setting Hollywood stars. The beautiful players upon the silver screen showed what was stylish and how to wear it. The jewelry of the 1940s and 1950s is highly collectible. Designs can be studied in the old movies where stars like Ava Gardner, Rita Hayworth, Paulette Goddard, Bette Davis, and Joan Crawford wore jewelry designs that are now legendary (Fig. 1–11).

**Fig. 1–11** *This two-color gold and ruby bracelet is a design from the Retro period. The double-snake-link straps border a series of gold concentric rings inset with twelve round faceted rubies. The bracelet is signed by John Rubel Company. (Courtesy C. G. Sloan & Co. Auctioneers. © Peter Harholdt Studio.)*

Because platinum was needed for military purposes during the World War II years, a similar metal called palladium was substituted. However, it never gained the appeal of platinum. Mounting designs of the period are bold, oversized, and flamboyant. Costume jewelry with base metal and glass stones reached an all-time high in popularity, and many pieces of jewelry from this period are set with synthetic rubies, sapphires, or emeralds.

Although Retro jewelry is not antique in the purest sense, it is certainly collectible. If searching for it, whether it is finely crafted or costume jewelry, today's hunter will find a seemingly endless number of dealers devoted to the Retro era. The prices, while affordable today, are notably on the rise.

# RETRO-AT-A-GLANCE

## Motifs Most Frequently Found in Retro Jewelry

• Flowing scrolls • bows • knots • florals • hearts
• bows • arrows • small animals • insects • birds
• snakes

## Designs and Styles of Retro Jewelry

• Dramatic and bold designs • Heavy links in bracelets
• Charm bracelets with numerous charms
• Expansion arm bracelets • Large pendants of bold design
• Pendants that convert to brooches
• Hinged lockets with space inside for photographs

## Gemstones and Metals of the Retro Period

• Oversized citrines • smoky quartz • aquamarine • golden beryl
• tourmaline • peridot • amber • glass • synthetic ruby • sapphire • emerald • palladium • base metals • tricolor gold

# CHAPTER TWO

# $\mathcal{L}$ESSONS $\mathcal{F}$ROM THE $\mathcal{P}$ROFESSIONALS

## VIEWPOINTS AND TIPS
## FROM COLLECTORS

Where do you find it? How do you recognize it? What should you pay for it? What *must* you know about antique jewelry to keep from making a buying mistake? These questions and more were asked of collectors and antique-jewelry dealers willing to share their knowledge and expertise about the subject. One of the first rules of those who have been collecting for decades was "Know before you buy." All possible information about a particular item, time period or category of jewelry (Victorian bracelets, for example) should be gathered before the first purchase is made. Not only does having knowledge of a specific jewelry item help you avoid costly mistakes, it makes collecting more enjoyable.

The following advice was gleaned from both collectors and antique jewelry dealers in the United States and Europe:

❋ *What is the most important element to look for
in antique jewelry?*

Many dealers said, "Quality, condition, and rarity." Others
talked about good workmanship as an indicator of quality.
Fine workmanship deserves and commands a higher price
than shoddy craftsmanship, whether it is in precious or base
metal and whether it features gems or glass.

❋ *How do you assess condition besides just
looking at the item?*

"You can often feel it," was one dealer's advice. "Old pieces
have a softness of workmanship; and if you develop a tactile
sense, you can actually *feel* the condition of the jewelry." That is
not so esoteric as it sounds. Most old jewelry will not have
hard edges because it has been handled for many years. There
should be no little bits of metal sticking out from beneath a setting. If you put it side by side with new jewelry, you will soon
begin to decipher the "I am old" message it is sending. This
"feeling" becomes apparent with reproductions, says this dealer. "I have seen a lot of 15-karat Etruscan Revival-style gold
jewelry with crisp and hard edges, without wear, the granulation not finished off the way it should be, with the polish
unsure. In Art Deco reproductions, many of the millegrained
edges feel like sandpaper, while the genuine old Deco jewelry
millegrained edges have a smooth, almost silky feeling."

❋ *How can you tell value?*

By the quality and condition of a piece, by its integrity (it has
not been repaired or worked on to change it), and by its mar-
ketability.

There is no easy answer, dealers emphasized. It is no easier to tell the true value of a piece of antique jewelry at first
glance—certainly from the collector's point of view—than it
would be in fine art. There is so much more to antique jewelry than the  purely intrinsic (precious metals and gemstones)

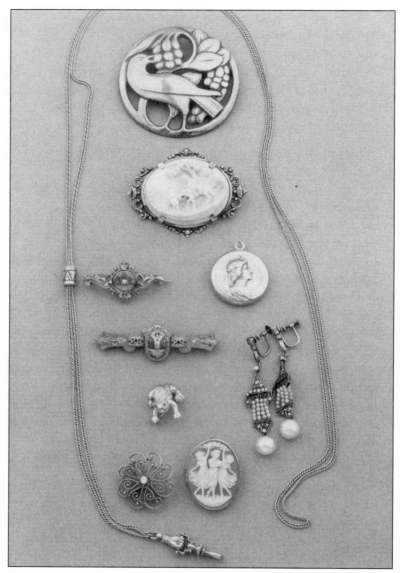

**Fig. 2–1** *A variety of antique and estate collectibles. Some collectors believe in putting money into design instead of metal or gems. (Courtesy C. G. Sloan & Co. Auctioneers. © Peter Harholdt Studio.)*

value. A piece of antique jewelry is *more* than its components, and a buyer must take design and provenance (origin) into consideration along with quality and condition.

"Don't put your money into the gemstones, but into the design," cautioned one collector. "The jewelry should be personal and something one will enjoy wearing repeatedly for years," she said, and added, "Look for something different." The collector used her own collection of mourning jewelry as an example of "different," advising looking for pieces with two tombstones instead of one, or with a departing ship or Grecian urn in the background. "But," she added as a final bit of advice, "be prepared to pay more for unusual jewelry pieces." See Figure 2–1.

❋ *Where are the best places to buy antique jewelry?*
"Because there is a big surge in the popularity of antique and estate jewelry, there is now an increased demand. So shop where the jewelry has always been most prevalent, if you can," one dealer told us. "In the United States, this means the Northeast; in Europe, this means London, Paris, and Amsterdam."

An American jewelry collector living in Europe is quick to point out that the best antique-jewelry hunting in the world is in London. The sheer number of stationary markets, each with forty, sixty, or one hundred dealers marks a happy hunting round. "If you are able to get to England, get a directory of antique dealers in London and visit those listed first," she said. "Some are prestigious, but their prices are outrageous. Some have tiny shops and some only one counter of jewelry; so, without a big overhead, they can be more generous with pricing. Look first, make notes, reflect upon what you have seen, and then return." In simple terms, do not rush into any transaction before you have time to study the items and their prices.

Other suggestions for finding good buys range from purchasing from private individuals to careful canvassing of flea markets. One dealer put it this way; "If you do not know anything about antique jewelry, buy from a reputable dealer who can educate you; if you do know antique jewelry, buy anywhere!" While you hear stories about somebody going into an antiques show, garage sale, or flea market and finding an obscure item for a few dollars that later turns out to be worth a fortune, you never believe it can happen to you, but it might! The author of an antique-jewelry price guide tells about buying a Russian bracelet at a flea market for a modest price that turned out—to his delight—to be a piece of Fabergé jewelry worth more than $20,000!

❀ *Why is antique jewelry suddenly in such demand?*
Because of broad forces that affect value such as social change, economic conditions, crime, and taxation.

Today's buyers want value in their collectibles. It is clear that antique jewelry has enduring value, especially if the piece is immediately wearable. Further, old jewelry has *hidden value* that many believe keeps away jewelry thieves; most collectors believe that burglars—and fences—neither know or care about old jewelry.

Taxes must be considered as a part of the buying or selling of jewelry. Today the United States government fines contemporary jewelry with a luxury tax that is not imposed on antique jewelry.

❀ *Is one type item of antique jewelry more collectible than another?*
Some dealers say that antique jewelry *rings* are in short supply because they are items most likely to have worn out. The more years a ring was worn and loved, the greater the chance of the shank becoming so thin that the piece is barely wearable.

"Buy earrings when you can get them," a dealer suggests. "Antique earrings are difficult to find because pairs were often divided between family members, or one of the pair was lost."

There is no shortage of either brooches or necklaces, and dealers point out that if antique jewelry is found in its original fitted box, both the desirability of the item and its value are increased.

Clever collectors can combine some categories of items under one subject heading to give strength to the overall appeal and value of their collections. For example, a Texas physician has mixed a vast accumulation of Victorian antique garnet jewelry with Sherlock Holmes memorabilia. The desire for gathering the garnet jewelry rose out of reports that Sherlock Holmes was born in January, so his birthstone was a garnet. Combining Holmes books, articles, and commemoratives with an impressive mass of garnet pins, rings, pendants, necklaces, earrings, and belt buckles has resulted in an unexpected plus for the physician. Besides being an expert on Sherlock Holmes, he has become a connoisseur of garnet gemstones used in the nineteenth century and expert at identifying and circa dating various clasps and other findings used in Victorian jewelry.

## PLAYING THE AUCTION GAME

Many people assume that a good place to find and buy antique jewelry is at regional, national, and international auctions. Well, yes and no. Yes, if you have done your homework and remember the requirements for buying at auction: knowledge of how to circa date, assess condition and value, and spot a reproduction. No, if you expect someone else to do the work for you and pick up unlimited bargains.

Auction buyers should understand that commercial auctions are not charitable institutions and that they exist to make money. They appear in a wide range of specialties and conditions, from the glittery and glamorous events of international Sotheby's and Christie's to country "junk" auctions. Regardless of status, auctions are socially acceptable and a legitimate way for the jewelry hunter to see both ends of the price spectrum from record-breaking highs to unbelievable bargains. Most beginning collectors find this market early in their hunt by pursuing auction catalogs and becoming enthused by the offerings.

Auction catalogs contain your first caveats, so beware. Study the catalog closely, *before you place your first bid.* Pay particular attention to the front matter in the book, concentrating on understanding the conditions of sale and glossary of terms. Frequently overlooked, this important information tells you how to be a good operator at auction.

Be familiar with the requirements of the auction house, and recognize that rules change from house to house. Along with the dates and times of the current auction, the catalog will tell you the names of the estates to be auctioned, or on whose behalf the items are being sold. It will explain the terms "bid price," "hammer price," "bidder's fee," "absentee bids," "reserves," and how the bidding will flow in increment multiples. The explanation of what the auction house considers "antique" is very important. The glossary will also explain what is meant by "style," "signed or stamped," "attributed," and "date/origin." You will find out the individual auction house's interpretation of the dates of various periods and what years are considered as encompassing Victorian, Art Deco, and so forth.

There are some auction houses with admission to sales

only if the attendees have a catalog of the sale. For instance, Sloan's Auction in Maryland warns in its catalog: "To attend an auction you *must* have a catalog or be with a person who does."

A prime reason to read the catalog before you bid is the important Limiting Conditions list which *all* auctions publish. Most of them simply use these caveats to buyers: "We do not guarantee the merchandise." And "Condition as is, where is." This is why it is vital for you to view the jewelry for auction personally, during the preauction viewing time, so you can carefully inspect the item's conditions. You cannot simply rely upon catalog descriptions or photographs. The photographs cannot be counted upon to show wear, broken or missing parts, repairs, or alterations. Although some catalogs may mention missing gemstones in a description, many will not. And, even with a glowing description in a catalog, upon actual viewing, the piece may differ from your mental picture. Before bidding you should be satisfied that the jewelry is from the period it is purported to be, is not a reproduction—or, if it is, the understanding of that fact—if it has been repaired or "married." (A "marriage" refers to the putting together of two or more parts from one period to create an entire but completely new piece of jewelry.)

It is important to know that most auction items have a "reserve," the minimum price agreed on by the consignor (owner of the jewelry) and the auction house for which the piece will be sold. Auction houses are likely to set this reserve as low as the client will permit in hopes that it will bring a much higher price, thus making the consignor happy. If the reserve is not reached during bidding, the auctioneer may "buy it in," or else withdraw it and simply move along to the next lot. Only the most astute of the auction crowd will even know that the item has not been sold. When a piece does sell, the buyer pays the "hammer price"—the price for which it sold—plus a buyer's premium, usually 10 percent of the sales price, and local taxes, if any.

It is a fine idea to keep all your old catalogs with their hammer prices even if you do not bid or buy, and file them away as part of your reference library.

## BUYER BEWARE

Even with a strong interest in antique jewelry, the savvy collector cannot depend upon luck, but must supplement knowledge with visits to museums, special exhibitions of designers and craftsmen (often held in boutiques or department stores), attendance at gem and mineral shows, and antique shows. Additional help can be found in technical-jewelry magazines such as *Jewellery Studies*, published by The Society of Jewellery Historians, U.K.; trade journals available to jewelers (in your local library), and mass-marketed antiques magazines. If your local bookstore carries antiques magazines from England, they are especially interesting, and will provide a European perspective on antique jewelry.

## AVOID MISTAKES

A checklist to avoid errors in judgment can be handy for both beginning and advanced collectors. There are at least 10 questions to ask yourself when buying antique jewelry. If you can answer yes to all of them you have greatly reduced your chances of purchasing a "mistake."

1. Is it wearable *as it is* on your body or clothes?

2. Is it stylistically correct for its purported period?

3. Is the style well defined? (A clearly defined item will be more valuable than a transitional one—i.e., between periods)

4. Are you satisfied with the circa date?

5. Have you asked about repairs? Guarantee?

6. Do rings fit without sizing? Clasps close properly? Bracelet hinges solid and tight?

7. Is the craftsmanship good to excellent?

8. If there are gemstones, have they been identified?

9. Are the gemstones secure in their settings?

10. Will the piece enhance (highlight or be an asset) to your collection?

And, a final bit of advice to beginning collectors: *Listen more. Ask more questions. Observe. Remember. Compare.*

## CHAPTER THREE

# THE WISE BUYER

## LEARNING THE LANGUAGE OF ANTIQUE JEWELRY

If antique jewelry has a language all its own, exactly what is it saying? You can tell a lot about a piece by observation and deduction. For instance, you have already read about circa dating using design clues and motifs of specific periods. There is also some jewelry vocabulary to remember (see Glossary), along with other design terms. For example, if you see the words *karat* and *carat* written or stamped upon a piece of jewelry (also written ct. or K), you can make an educated assumption that the item is European or American. In European antique goods, especially English, the metal content of an item is indicated with either the word *carat* or letter "c." In the United States, the fineness of gold is expressed in *karats* (24 karat is pure gold), and the word *carat* refers to weight in gemstones. A decimal system is also used to indicate gold fineness; i.e., .585 = 14 karat; .750 = 18 karat. The decimal system is most often found on European-made goods.

## GEMSTONES

The gemstones themselves have something to reveal, and it is up to you to know the language. With twentieth-century technology, it is easy to make copies look like genuine antiques. Man-made cubic zirconia or CZ, faceted in antique rose-cuts or old European cuts, can easily be passed to the unwary as genuine antique-cut diamonds (Fig. 3–1).

Collectors of antique jewelry must understand the following terminology:

*Natural stone:* A gemstone that was mined or taken out of the ground. Other than cutting and possibly faceting, the stone has not been altered.

*Enhanced stone:* This is a natural stone that may have been treated in a variety of ways to help it look better by improving either its clarity, color, or both. The methods used may be heat, oil, or dye, and the processes are *usually* irreversible. For centuries, stones like ruby, sapphire, aquamarine and others have been heat treated to deepen

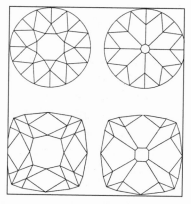

**Fig. 3–1** *Learn the language of gemstones. Top: Old-European cut; bottom, Old-mine cut. Note that the Old-mine cut has a squarer (cushion) outline, while the Old-European-cut stone is rounder, with a small table facet.*

their color. Also, for years, emeralds have been oiled (usually with clear or green-tinted oil) to fill their fractures and fissures. Jade is dyed to enhance its color and bring a higher price (particularly lavender), and lapis lazuli is dyed to a deep blue color. A current technique of high-tech society is the irradiation of white topaz to turn it a brilliant blue. This dazzling shade of blue topaz should not be found in a piece of Victorian jewelry and, if identified as such, indicates that it is not the original stone. A list of gemstones found in antique jewelry is given at the end of this chapter.

*Stabilized:* This refers to a treatment which alters a gemstone to the extent that it is no longer the same substance, and *it is legal.* Because turquoise is a major gem that is stabilized, it is one that you will want to look at carefully when you find it in antique jewelry. In stabilization, turquoise of poor quality is crushed, reformed, and soaked in an acrylic bath, and sometimes color enhanced. Many gemstones are dyed to improve the color; sometimes pale transparent stones are painted on their backs to increase their color and brilliance.

*Synthetic stones:* Natural gemstones are those unique creations of Mother Nature, while synthetic gemstones are grown in laboratories. However, the synthetics have the same physical, chemical, and optical properties as their natural counterparts; the only difference is that they all have been created by man.

Synthetic stones might be found in some antique jewelry since the first ruby synthetics were introduced into the market in 1885 and were prevalent through 1905. In 1920 synthetic sapphires came into use; synthetic emeralds followed in the early 1930s. Many people have in their possession what they believe to be natural rubies, sapphires, or emeralds because they once belonged to their grandmothers. "It must be natural," they protest, "because granddad would *never* have bought it if it was not a natural gemstone!" The reality is that in all probability granddad did not *know* it was not natural, and neither did the jeweler who sold it to him. When the first synthetics came into the market, the knowledge or desire to identify them was not of any great importance. And synthetics, unlike glass, were not cheap, so their relationship to natural gemstones was not as easily understood by the average buyer. Synthetics can take months and sometimes years to grow in a laboratory. However, because they are infinitely reproducible, they do cost less than nature's own gems. Today synthetic diamonds, first introduced in 1905, have come under close scrutiny since the disclosure of their commercial production by the Japanese. Until recently it was felt that the only synthetic diamonds being produced were utilized by industry. Sumitomo Electric Industries advanced both the quality and quantity of gem-quality synthetic diamonds during the 1980s. DeBeers has also revealed that it has been researching and developing synthetic diamonds since the 1970s. Buyers and sellers of contemporary and antique jewelry may soon have to ask for a certificate of authentication as well as identification on gemstones and jewelry.

*Imitations:* Imitation gemstones have existed from the earliest times that men and women began to adorn themselves. Today they range from colored plastics and glass that look like precious colored gems, to pearls and diamonds.

There are a number of misleading names in gemstones. These are sometimes used with genuine materials, sometimes with imitation materials:

| *Misleading Name* | *What It Really Is* |
|---|---|
| Evening emerald | Peridot |
| Oriental emerald | Green sapphire |
| African jade | Green garnet |
| Mexican jade | Dyed green calcite |
| Cape ruby | Garnet |

| Misleading Name | What It Really Is |
|---|---|
| Balas ruby | Spinel |
| Swiss jade | Dyed green jasper |
| Swiss lapis | Dyed blue jasper |
| Smoky topaz | Brown quartz |
| Madeira topaz | Citrine quartz |
| German lapis | Dyed blue jasper |
| Goldstone | Man-made glass with copper particles |

*Doublets and Triplets:* These are composite stones made up of two or three pieces of material to look like something they are not. *They are made to deceive.* In the United States jewelry market, "doublet" refers to a sandwichlike stone created by bonding two pieces of material together with a colorless glue; a "triplet" refers to two pieces of material joined together with a colored bonding agent (colored gelatin or other substance) in the center, or three pieces of material sandwiched together (Fig. 3–2) to create one gemstone. This deception is not new; both doublets and triplets have been around for a long time. They were especially prevalent in the Late Victorian era, around the turn of the century. The most popular type of doublets found in antique jewelry (although *anything* is and can be found) are

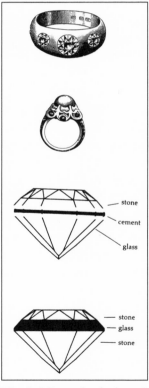

**Fig. 3–2** *Example of a faceted gemstone, a cabochon-cut stone, doublet, and a triplet.*

garnet doublets consisting of a stone with a thin portion of red garnet fused to glass at the top. The garnet is used at the top because of its luster and durability. Incredible though it seems, the garnet's natural red color does not affect the color of the faux gemstone it portrays. If, for example, the glass on the bottom of the stone is deep green, the red of the garnet will not be seen, nor will it be obvious to the viewer. The stone will look all green! There are various combinations of doublets: those with genuine composite parts, some genuine, some glass, some other materials. However, all are created to make you think you are seeing something that is not there. It is a magic show.

Most poor-quality natural sapphires with synthetic corundum bases cemented onto them, as well as sapphires onto which a blue layer has been fused, are obvious doublets, but they are difficult to detect if they are set, especially in bezels.

The importance of obtaining positive identification on gems cannot be overemphasized. Do not make assumptions of identification based on what *appears* to be the age of the jewelry, the asking price, or the reputation of the former owner or dealer who has it for sale. A good example of the danger inherent in assumption is provided by the auction of the Duchess of Windsor's jewels at Sotheby's in Geneva, Switzerland in April 1987. A strand of pearls listed as cultured turned out to be simulated (imitation). Someone *assumed* they were fine-quality cultured pearls because they had belonged to the duchess.

Part of learning the language of jewelry is answering the question "What is it?" You may or may not want to add a muff chain to a growing collection of neck chains. This question leads to another; "How was it used?" During the Victorian era, ladies wore hunting-case watches around their necks on long decorative chains. Most chains were decorated with a slide that allowed the wearer to adjust the watch to a

**Fig. 3–3** *(left) A Victorian chain with slide on a hunting-case watch.*

**Fig. 3–4** *(right) Slides were produced in a great variety of styles and designs during the Victorian era. Today they are collected and worn together on attractive bracelets like the one pictured. These slides have been dated to 1880 and are probably English. (Courtesy Elizabeth Pierce Green.)*

desired length (Fig. 3–3). Today these slides are collected and displayed on bracelets (Fig. 3–4). Understanding of the original way in which they were worn increases the enjoyment of the collection.

One of the questions your jewelry should answer by its workmanship and condition is how it ranks as an example of its type. A lot of looking and handling of antique jewelry is necessary before you will gain expertise in what is good, better, or best of its kind.

# THE MOST BASIC TOOL
## AND HOW TO USE IT

You learn to identify and class antique jewelry by sight and later taste, touch, and smell. Sight, especially magnified sight, becomes the most important of the five senses from the very first purchase. All buyers, collectors, and connoisseurs of antique jewelry—whether they are beginners or advanced collectors—should know how to use a jeweler's magnifying lens, or loupe (Fig. 3–5), as it is called in the trade. Further, the use of one should be so natural and automatic that it becomes one

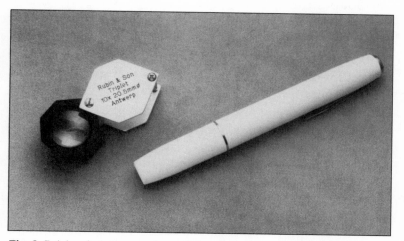

**Fig. 3–5** *A jeweler's loupe and a penlight are the two most valuable tools for the collector to purchase and learn how to use.*

tool you *always* carry in your pocket or purse. Many people try to use a loupe without any idea of how to handle it properly and, while many will not admit it, they end up not being able to see clearly through the lens. Of course, additional study is needed to know *what* you are looking for (and expect to see) once you have mastered the tool. A *triplet-lens* jeweler's loupe is the most important tool in your arsenal; buy one before you make your first purchase of antique jewelry.

A loupe is a special kind of magnifying lens that comes in various powers of magnification from six-power (6X) to twenty-four-power (24X). The principle is simple; a 6X loupe presents an image six times larger than the subject being viewed; 10X ten times; 14X fourteen times, and so forth. The most often used power of magnification is 10X; a triplet-lens is most desired because it will have been corrected for visual distortion (spherical aberration), in which the edges of the lens distort the image, and color (chromatic) distortion, in which traces of color are seen at the edges of the lens. Triplet-lens loupes can be purchased at jeweler's supply houses. Consult your Yellow Pages.

When mastered, the loupe is a practical and valuable tool to examine hallmarking and details of workmanship, to inspect for repairs, chips, or cracks, and to inspect gemstones for inclusions or fractures. A loupe can also help the user spot reproductions, imitations, and knock-off replicas.

Handling a loupe is not difficult, but it may take some practice, and the entire process may feel a bit clumsy until it has been tried several times.

Here are the basic steps to using a magnifying loupe, including the correct posture.

1. Hold the loupe between your thumb and forefinger. Do not hold it by its lens, but rather by its housing or handle.

2. Hold the jewelry in your other hand.

3. Brace the arm and hand in which you hold the loupe tightly against your chest in order to steady the tool.

4. Put the loupe close to your eye. You do not have to remove your glasses, just rest the loupe against the eyeglass lens.

5. Try to keep both eyes open when looking through the loupe.

6. Slowly bring the jewelry (or gem) you are examining into view by moving it *toward the loupe* (the loupe is still at your eye) until it comes into sharp focus. The critical focus area will probably be no more than 1 inch from the loupe.

7. Move and tilt the *jewelry or gem* (not the loupe) around for various angles and observations. Practice moving the object back and forth toward the loupe until you have established the sharpest focus you can manage for your eye. It takes patience and practice.

Some people mistakenly assume that the higher the power of a loupe, the better. Actually, using higher magnification than 10X is more difficult and completely unnecessary for the average jewelry collector. It is more difficult because higher magnification makes the viewing field smaller; also, the higher the degree of magnification, the shorter the focus and smaller the depth of field. Beginners often find it difficult to understand exactly what they are supposed to be seeing anyway; therefore, by using a higher magnification than necessary and shortening your field of vision, you may miss many revealing elements.

Interestingly enough, some unethical dealers do understand how difficult it is to master use of a very-high-powered loupe and use this knowledge to try and confuse the buyer by offering a 20X or higher lens to look through. The wily dealer knows that almost no one will turn down the opportunity to try the loupe, or, when customers do try, confess that they cannot see clearly through the lens. Instead, customers are all too often inclined to play along with the nod of a head and a mumbled "uh-huh."

## OPTIONAL EQUIPMENT

Good light that floods the surface of the jewelry or gemstone under examination is an absolute necessity for the buyer. Most antique shops and some commercial antique shows fail to provide adequate light in which to examine gemstones and jewelry. Serious buyers overcome that nuisance by carrying their own penlights in a pocket or purse. The penlight is used along with the loupe for careful scrutiny of jewelry. After all, jewelry buyers are still universally reminded of the traditional warning "caveat emptor"—buyer beware—and need all the advantages they can mobilize.

## IS YOUR JEWELRY MARRIED?

One of the most important uses of your loupe is to enable you to judge an item's condition. When you pick up a piece of jewelry, examine the back carefully and look for signs of wear, breaks, metal tears, or burrs of metal sticking out from places where they should not be. You can determine if the piece has been damaged or altered from its original state by close observation. Look at the item from all angles and examine how the gemstones are mounted. You may be able to recognize different stylistic periods in one piece of jewelry. This "marriage" is common in antique jewelry and creates strong devaluation of the piece.

*Note:* Signs of wear on ring shanks and pin stems are normal. In fact, gold-plated pieces may show the base metal through the plating due to wear. If a piece is purported to be old but shows no signs of wear, a red flag should go up in your mind. Ask the dealer *why* it shows no wear. It may be that it has been repolished, or that it is a reproduction.

# HOW TO TELL
## A REPRODUCTION

In the year A.D. 77, the Roman historian Pliny the Elder wrote in his thirty-seventh book *History of the World*, commonly called *Naturalis Historia*:

"To tell the truth, there is no fraud or deceit in the world which yields greater gain and profit than that of counterfeiting gems."

It is still true, and today we can add, *along with counterfeiting jewelry*. A *reproduction* is a type of counterfeit. In his *Illustrated Dictionary of Jewelry*, author Harold Newman defines a reproduction as a close copy of a genuine article made without intent to deceive. It might be a copy of a piece made at a prior date with the same design and materials by the original maker and sold without intention to deceive. *Webster's Third International Dictionary* calls a reproduction "an exact copy."

It is impossible to write about antique jewelry without mentioning the vast quantity of reproductions that *are* made to deceive, along with the outright forgeries and fakes. Many pieces are so well replicated they cannot be readily identified as such; they present problems to both new and experienced collectors as well as to dealers, jewelers, and gemologists.

Forgeries, usually identical, or closely similar to the genuine article, are made especially to deceive. Fakes are counterfeits or imitations (often poorly done) presented—with fraudulent intent—as genuine.

Because of the demand for classical antiquities, including jewelry, all past eras have had their share of fakes. Jewelry makers had plenty of dealers willing to sell their products. In the Middle Ages, even sacred relics were faked because they were so desired by the nobility and laypersons; and, regretfully, there were monks willing to traffic in faked sacred relics, crosses and other religious items.

Gloria Lieberman, head of the jewelry department at Skinner's, a major New England auction house in Boston, says that *everything* has been reproduced, with at least 90 percent of all the antique jewelry seen today "reproduced or altered in some form." Further, she warns, "Reproductions get better and better as time goes by."

One of the reasons for the difficulty in differentiating reproductions from originals is that many companies today have recalled into use the original antique jewelry molds and models, along with the old manufacturing methods. Some companies make the antique look a specialty line. Reproductions and fakes are almost national exports from some countries like Portugal and Germany. Fakes made in the Middle East and Asia are screened with a degree of secrecy; once the pieces get into the chain of buyers and sellers, they acquire less of the label as "fake" and become harder to identify.

Some fakes with apparent authentic background are moved through international auction houses or dealers. Antiquities in gold, silver, and other materials, that are claimed to date from ancient Egypt or medieval Britain, have been faked in large quantities in the last few decades. Further, some chemical processes have been developed by fakers for the patination of metals and aging of gemstones that have resulted in fooling even museum experts and connoisseur collectors.

Lieberman tells collectors to think about weight in the genuinely old jewelry, as a lot of old jewelry is constructed solidly and is heavier than its reproduction counterparts. Another clue that the piece may be a reproduction is its scale. "The reproduction Victorian bangle bracelets on the market from the 1950s production," Lieberman says, "are usually much larger than their counterparts, the true Victorians, and they are frequently florentined, a finish not found on the old bangles."

Some other tips to use in differentiating antiques from reproductions:

1. In antiques, the backs of the jewelry should be well finished, even under any existing enamel.

2. In antiques, engraving on the backs will be well done and complete, and without a "hurried" look seen in the reproduction.

3. In antiques, cuts and kind of gemstones will be correct for the period.

4. In reproductions, the pieces may *look* heavy, but may be only hollow Asian-made replicas.

5. Reproductions will show lack of wear.

6. In reproductions, the patina is too perfect; the piece has a pristine look.

A critical reason to learn your way around this market—regardless of whether the jewelry was made to deceive, or just an honest attempt at revival—has to do with price. Prices of the reproductions should differ from the genuine antiques: sometimes higher, sometimes lower. It may depend upon the gemstones used and the price of labor today that raises the cost of a reproduction well beyond the price of its genuine counterpart. Or, for the genuine article, you are paying for a specific style, period, and quality of work that the reproduction simply *cannot* duplicate, and the antique's price reflects these elements of value.

Some collectors believe that one way to spot a reproduction is by the sheer numbers of identical pieces in the market, and that theory does hold up.

Because of cycles of taste and demand in some years you will find a vast array of one type of antique jewelry on the market. Then it seems to disappear and is replaced by another trend. Therefore, when you see large numbers of one type of item on the market, your suspicions should be aroused.

Also, if designer pieces, such as by Fabergé are found in

antique shops at prices far below what they should bring, be a wary buyer. Do not be fooled into thinking that the dealer is not knowledgeable about such a world-famous designer, or is doing you a favor on the price. Lynette Proler, an antique jewelry dealer in Houston, says that Fabergé jewelry will *never* be found priced under several thousand dollars. Proler warns that you should be apprehensive of "deals" because it is illogical for a dealer to sell you—a stranger—a genuine Fabergé brooch for a few hundred dollars when, if it is genuine, it will bring several times the price at auction.

There is a lot of reproduction and fake Fabergé jewelry around. A few years ago at a gems and jewelry show in Tucson, a dealer covered a tabletop with what he called "genuine Fabergé." When someone asked him if it was signed, he answered candidly and calmly, "Not yet."

## LEARNING TO JUDGE QUALITY, STYLE, AND WORKMANSHIP

A well-made piece of antique jewelry is beautiful front and back, and appears strong even if it is made delicately. The detail of its modeling should be sharp and clean; solder joints should not be seen; its finish will be executed finely. Pieces in the best condition will be priced higher than their shabby counterparts. And, it is unquestionably true that the more beautifully made a piece is, the more expensive it will be to repair, should repair be needed.

While collectors should find a noticeable price difference between poorly made and well-made antique jewelry, that may not always be the reality. Some dealers see only the word "antique" and take it as a license for higher prices. A lot of antique jewelry is sold today and priced only on its style or period. Therefore, it is up to you to educate yourself about quality.

A lesson quickly learned is that the more you get to know about gemstones' quality, the less acceptable you will find poor-quality gemstones. And, if the colored gems in your jewelry have serious problems, like chips or cracks, the less lovable those pieces will be to you the longer you own them.

## THESE GEMSTONES ARE COMMONLY FOUND SET IN ANTIQUE JEWELRY

| | |
|---|---|
| Amber | Carnelian |
| Agate | Diamond |
| Seed pearls | Jade |
| Pink topaz | Natural pearls |
| Coral | Jet |
| Blue topaz (pale) | Aquamarine |
| Tortoiseshell | Opal |
| Ivory | Malachite |
| Red garnet | Green demantoid garnet |
| Lapis lazuli | Onyx |
| Ruby | Synthetic Ruby |
| Peridot | Turquoise |
| Sapphire | Tourmaline |
| Emerald | Zircon |
| Amethyst | Alexandrite |
| Lava | |

## THESE GEMSTONES WOULD NOT BE FOUND IN ANTIQUE JEWELRY

If they are found in pieces of antique jewelry, they have probably been substituted for the original gemstone.

| | |
|---|---|
| Tanzanite | Tsavorite |
| Red beryl | Charoite |
| Benitoite | Taaffeite |
| "London Blue" topaz | Cultured pearls |
| Turquoise in matrix | Kunzite |
| Sugilite | Syn. Spinel |
| Syn. Opal | Syn. Coral |
| Syn. Turquoise | Syn. Lapis lazuli |
| Strontium Titanate | Cubic Zirconia(CZ) |
| Syn. Corundum | GGG-Gadolinium |
| YAG-Yttrium | gallium garnet |
| aluminum garnet | Syn. Sapphire |
| Syn. Alexandrite | Syn. Citrine |
| Syn. Quartz | Syn. Ametrine |
| Syn. Amethyst | Rhodochrosite |
| Syn. Jadeite | Fracture-filled gems |
| Irradiated gemstones | Heat-treated corundum |
| Stabilized turquoise | |

# REPAIRS AFFECT VALUE

A classic rule for collectors is "Buy only what you like." Then, if you pay too much, at least it is for an item that you admire and want to live with. The cardinal rule for antique-jewelry buyers is to buy only items you like *that are in good condition*; or, if minor repairs are needed, they can be obtained without major cost.

Most enamel jewelry cannot be repaired easily because enamel is glass and is therefore easily damaged. It must be

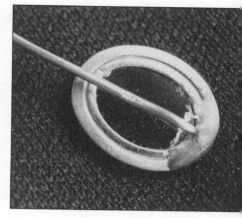

Fig. 3–6 *A poor repair job with gobs of lead solder devalues a piece.*

melted to be repaired, and any "repair" may damage existing enamel. If it *can* be repaired, it is often a very expensive process.

Repair or replacement of worn or missing settings can be costly, so inspect closely before you buy. A good practice is to insist upon a detailed written receipt and the right to return goods if you later find them not what you were led to believe. Soft lead or tin solder repairs are so damaging to the value of a piece of jewelry that often they may be devalued by half or more (Fig. 3–6).

The bottom line is that if a piece has missing parts, damaged enamel, poor settings, or has had parts such as pin stems replaced with blobs of gray solder, pass it by.

## CHAPTER FOUR

# What Is Affordable?

"What is available?" and "Where can I find affordable antique jewelry?" are questions frequently asked at antique-jewelry seminars. Answers are not easily found and, when given, they are usually complicated because of the highly personal nature of the jewelry sought.

Although the majority of the collectible antique jewelry for sale in the market today is of European origin, some late-eighteenth- and early-nineteenth-century American items do exist. Finding them, though, requires a concentrated search in markets known to be rich in other kinds of early American memorabilia; cities like Boston and Philadelphia in the North, and New Orleans, Charleston and Atlanta in the South. Old American jewelry is scarce: families proud of their heritage normally passed pieces from generation to generation, and many heirs have never felt the need to sell. Lockets, beads, cape clasps, brooches, and earrings were divided among daughters who may have moved to far away locations, and

**Fig. 4–1** *(above left) A man's engraved amethyst and gold ring, from the Von Schweintz family, circa 1780. (Courtesy Old Salem, Inc.)*

**Fig. 4–2** *(above right) Gimmel gold wedding ring circa 1819. (Courtesy Old Salem, Inc.*

**Fig. 4–3** *(right) A pair of English gold and black enamel bracelets, dated 1880. (Courtesy Old Salem, Inc.)*

some pieces were lost, damaged, or destroyed. Jewelry is scattered around the country, in silent testimony to the restless migration of the people.

Museums have absorbed some of the old American jewelry, and collectors determined to build in this category will profit by viewing exhibits like those of the Moravians (a religious sect) in Old Salem, North Carolina. The Moravians, who arrived there in 1753, had a well-defined sense of history; they took pains to preserve written records of the use and manufacture of jewelry, along with the jewelry itself. The result is documentation that assists today's jewelry collector and historian trying to find provenance and to circa-date style and design.

The majority of pieces in the Old Salem collection were made by silversmith/gunsmith/watchmaker John Vogler

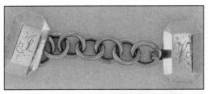

**Fig. 4–4** *(top) A silver cape clasp, engraved with a J on the left half and a V on the right. Made by John Vogler, circa 1820. (Courtesy Wachovia Historical Society.)*

**Fig. 4–5** *(bottom) An octagonal silver cape clasp, each side engraved with "H," circa 1820. (Courtesy Old Salem, Inc.)*

(1783–1881) in the mid-nineteenth century. It consists of rings (Figs. 4–1, 4–2), bracelets (Fig. 4–3), brooches, necklaces, earrings, and functional cape clasps (Figs. 4–4, 4–5).

While most museums have authenticated their collections with documentation, oral histories are not acceptable provenance—at least, not for most jewelry buyers. Buyers should listen thoughtfully but take a seller's story of the origin and past ownership of an item (where no written documentation exists), with the proverbial grain of salt.

An example of how well-meaning people can embellish or create the provenance of jewelry in order to enhance the selling price is illustrated in a recent case where an appraisal for resale was being written for two elderly sisters in Georgia. The appraiser went to their home, a fine old southern mansion, to examine the jewelry. The pair immediately began to lecture the appraiser on the quality and condition of the items, as well as their romantic provenance. The sisters spoke of how, during the Civil War, old family retainers hid the family jewels from the maurauding Yankee soldiers, how the family suffered during Sherman's march through Georgia, and how the jewelry was buried and therefore saved. Not only fascinating background but value making as well. In time, however, the appraiser had to discount the story as pure fabrication. Faint hallmarks on the jewelry gave away the fact that it was manufactured at the turn of the century, several decades *after* the end of the Civil War.

Sometimes the attempt at provenance can provide some very amusing incidents at the dealer's-market level. A jewelry-and-coin dealer at a recent traveling-jewelry show was touting "genuine" old Greek coins to be used in making jewelry. Upon closer inspection, however, stamped at the bottom of the coins under the profile of Alexander the Great was the startling legend in English: 500 B.C.

It is impossible to point out every collectible item of affordable antique jewelry available in the market today, but the following overview of affordable jewelry items will furnish a beginning.

## BRACELETS

The wearing of a bracelet is rooted in the arm rings of plaited or woven grasses, bones, and shells, worn by primitive men and women. What may initially have been a symbol of sympathetic magic was also used as body decoration, sometimes at the same time.

Early Egyptians, Greeks, and Assyrians knew plain and enameled metal bracelets, coiled spirals, and trumpet-end designs. Romans wore several bracelets on the right wrist and another one on the upper right arm. Some Victorians would wear up to five bracelets at the same time. Today many Middle Eastern women count their wealth by the number of 22-karat gold bangle bracelets they wear on one arm.

**Fig. 4–6** *(left) Enduring favorites, priced $800–$1,600: diamond and synthetic sapphire straightline bracelet, circa 1930; Victorian coral bracelet; an Edwardian platinum, diamond and sapphire bracelet. (Courtesy C. G. Sloan & Co. Auctioneers. © Peter Harholdt Studio.)*

**Fig. 4–7** *(right) English gold bangle bracelets dated from 1865, priced $1,500 up. The Assyrian-style gold and enamel bangle, circa 1872, has a twin in the British Museum. (Courtesy Lynette Proler Antiques.)*

Affluence is perceived as having gold bracelets marching from wrist to elbow.

Bangles (Fig. 4–6) seem to be the most enduring bracelet style. They reached a pinnacle of popularity during the Victorian era. The high-relief, enameled design of the bracelet in Figure 4–7 has the typical Assyrian-style motif that was registered with the British Patent Office in 1872 by J. F. Backes and Company. The Backes designs have been described as Victorian translations of ancient Assyrian sculptures found

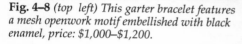

**Fig. 4–8** *(top left) This garter bracelet features a mesh openwork motif embellished with black enamel, price: $1,000–$1,200.*

**Fig. 4–9** *(right) The serpent-motif bracelet, center, $1,200 has been popular since early Greek and Roman days. Gold and lapis lazuli flexible snake-motif bracelet, left, is $700–$800; top, 14K gold and diamond Retro bangle, $1,800. (Courtesy C. G. Sloan & Co. Auctioneers. © Peter Harholdt Studio.)*

**Fig. 4–10** *(left)Antique and estate bracelets, many set with gemstones, can still be found at affordable prices. These, from $750 to $1,500: from left; Victorian gold and seen pearl bangle bracelet; 14K yellow gold, diamond and turquoise bangle; gold flexible link bracelet; yellow-gold-mesh Victorian bracelet. (Courtesy C. G. Sloan & Co., Auctioneers. © Peter Harholdt Studio.)*

during Sir Austen Layard's archaeological excavations of Nineveh in the 1840s. According to jewelry expert Lynette Proler, the bracelet seen in Figure 4–7 is only the second of these designs to have been found in over 100 years; the first is on exhibit in the British Museum.

Typical of the Victorian era are bracelets in the form of garters (Fig. 4–8) and serpents (Fig. 4–9). The garter motif seems to have originated around 1850 and was known as *jarretiere*, after the French word for garter. The design was used in many countries including America. As with a real garter,

**Fig. 4–11** *(left) Pictured are variations on the straight-line bracelet, from left: a 1930s platinum and diamond bracelet; an antique platinum, diamond and sapphire bracelet $1,750; Art Deco diamond straightline; and a turn-of-the-century platinum, diamond, and sapphire bracelet. Three are priced over our "affordable" limit, but reproductions of these styles can be found for a few hundred dollars. (Courtesy C. G. Sloan & Co., Auctioneers. © Peter Harholdt Studio.)*

**Fig. 4–12** *(right) A beautiful Victorian hinged oval onyx, rose gold, and seed pearl bangle bracelet. Panels of black onyx are set in beaded gold framers; It has a buckle motif, inset with seed pearls. Affordably priced at $600–$750. (Courtesy C. G. Sloan & Co. Auctioneers. © Peter Harholdt Studio.)*

the width of the opening of such a bracelet is altered by adjusting the clasp. The serpent was an important motif in Greek, Roman, and Victorian jewelry. Queen Victoria had a serpent-design bracelet she loved and wore often, and her engagement ring was also a serpent design. The symbolism was life-or love-everlasting.

At its simplest, a bracelet may be a chain with a clasp, or a thin wire ring slipped over the hand onto the wrist. At its most complex, it will have a clasp or hinge, be made of precious metal, and ornamented either with rolled-on decoration, gemstones, or enamel (Figs. 4–10, 4–11, 4–12).

Bracelets have gone in and out of fashion depending on the length of the garment sleeve, as well as the fashion for showing or hiding of the hands, and the fluctuating fortunes

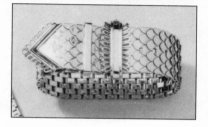

**Fig. 4–13** *(above)This lovely 18K antique bracelet, circa 1890, may be French. Priced over $3,000.*

**Fig. 4–14** *(top right) Jewelry should be examined closely for alterations. This bracelet may have once been hinged and now the ends have been sealed. (Courtesy P. J. Abramson.)*

**Fig. 4–15** *(bottom right) This late-Victorian bracelet has a garter motif. Revivals of this style can be found priced from $650. (Courtesy Lynette Proler Antiques.)*

of the middle class.

During the sixteenth century, pomander bracelets composed of filigree beads with perfume inside were popular. The preference for them undoubtedly grew from the lack of sanitary conditions and infrequent bathing. Bracelets were out of fashion in the seventeenth century and for most of the eighteenth century, but returned in the nineteenth. At the end of the 1800s, bracelets grew increasingly narrow until they began to lose their popularity,

For the most part, antique bangle bracelets—especially those of the Victorian era—have a diameter too small for modern wrists. Therefore, be sure to try on the bracelet before buying so that you can see that it fits comfortably over your hand, and it does not hug your wrist too tightly, nor fall down too far upon your hand. Precisely because many

**Fig. 4–16** *(left) Retro examples of affordable estate pieces: 14K yellow gold link bracelet, $1,400; an 18K cuff bracelet, circa 1940, $1,250– $1,750. (Courtesy C. G. Sloan & Co. Auctioneers. © Peter Harholdt Studio.)*

**Fig. 4–17** *(top) Silver can often be a good buy: silver, marcasite, and amethyst bracelet, $400. (Courtesy C. G. Sloan & Co. Auctioneers. © Peter Harholdt Studio.)*

**Fig. 4–18** *(right)Sterling-silver bracelets with silver heart charms, collectible in the 1930s and early 1940s, are now priced between $400 and $650.*

women have difficulty in getting a bangle bracelet over their hands, they prefer hinged bangles. However, even these can hug the wrist too tightly and look and feel uncomfortable. Try before you buy (Figs. 4–13, 4–14, 4–15).

Even though antique bracelets come in many designs, they will all exhibit one common element if they have been worn frequently: wear. Some may show damage, but all should show signs of wear, especially on hinges and clasps. Dents in hollow bangle bracelets are common. Unfortunately, they cannot be repaired successfully, so pass these bangles by.

Check the links in chain bracelets because they grow extremely thin at contact points, where one link touches another (Figs. 4–16, 4–17).

A major collectible today is the sterling-silver charm bracelet (Fig. 4–18) of the early twentieth century, particularly those with many hearts. These were especially popular just prior to World War II, when each sterling-silver heart could be bought for about 25 cents; today such a charm costs $10–$20.

## BROOCHES

Where did the first brooch come from? Nobody knows, but it is certain that it was some type of device used to hold clothing together. The first brooch probably originated around 1000 B.C. in the European Bronze Age and was a safety-pin-like device known as a fibula (Fig. 4–19). This design was still in use as late as the Middle Ages. It was followed by designs of the circular brooch, penannular brooch, and ring brooch (Figs. 4–20, 4–21, 4–22).

Early brooches had to fulfill specific functions on clothing: to fasten a collar to a dress, to close an opening, or to gather material into soft folds. Only later in the thirteenth century, when society's growing wealth was reflected in the goldsmith's art, did brooches take on the ornamentation provided by the large cloak clasp and dainty agraffe, a hook-and-loop type of fastening.

The forerunner of the modern brooch is reported to have been an ornament owned by Madame de Sévigné, a French aristocrat who wore a brooch in the design of a floppy bow not only as a garment clasp but to direct attention to her plunging décolleté.

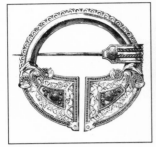

**Fig. 4–19** *(top left)The ancient fibula, forerunner of the brooch. (Courtesy Dover Publications.)*

**Fig. 4–20** *( center left) The ring brooch was designed as a circle with a hinged pin slightly longer than the diameter of the brooch. Used from medieval times, revivals of this style are common. (Courtesy Dover Publications.)*

**Fig. 4–21** *(above right) Estate jewelry: gold and diamond iris pin, bottom left, $750; Art Deco enamel and diamond circle pins, $800– $1,500; diamond brooches in classic styles, over the affordable limit. (Courtesy C. G. Sloan & Co. Auctioneers. © Peter Harholdt Studio.)*

**Fig. 4–22** *(left) Etruscan Revival style brooch, 15K with filigree and turquoise. A locket is on the reverse, $550. (Photo by Peggy Blackford.)*

In the eighteenth century, motifs of flowers, branches, bows, and garlands encrusted with diamonds were the fashion for brooches. At the end of the century, miniature portraits set into frames of pearls were used along with cameos set with semiprecious gemstones.

During the 1830s, some Gothic-style brooches called Berlin Iron—cast from iron—were fashionable wear after the Napoleonic Wars. Found primarily in Germany and France, the problem today is not the price, but finding the articles

**Fig. 4–23** *(left) Bird and animal brooches were popular from the middle 1800s. Typical are these 18K yellow gold pins, from $400. (Courtesy C. G. Sloan & Co. Auctioneers. © Peter Harholdt Studio.)*

**Fig. 4–24** *(center) Etruscan style Revival brooches in gold, priced from $100. (Courtesy Elizabeth Pierce Green.)*

**Fig. 4–25** *( top right) English 15K bar pin with two micromosaic panels, offered in its original fitted box, $350. (Courtesy C. G. Sloan & Co. Auctioneers. © Peter Harholdt Studio.)*

**Fig. 4–26** *This (center right) Victorian gold brooch has micromosaic decoration in a floral-spray motif, $400–$600. (Courtesy C. G. Sloan & Co. Auctioneers. © Peter Harholdt Studio.)*

**Fig. 4–27** *(bottom right) This micromosaic brooch has been altered and given new life as a clasp, $425. (Courtesy P. J. Abramson)*

intact and in good condition.

In the 1860s, brooch designs centered on Egyptian and Etruscan style revivals; medieval themes, and Scottish cairngorm or pebble jewelry. From about 1870 to the end of the century, the most popular designs were animals, insects, ships, wheels, musical instruments, flowers, and foliage (Figs. 4–23, 4–24).

The Victorian era was the golden age of the brooch, and a principal trend in brooch design was the archaeological styles

THE BUYER'S GUIDE TO AFFORDABLE ANTIQUE JEWELRY

**Fig. 4–29** *(above) An exceptionally fine Victorian shell cameo in a yellow-gold-filigree frame, $800. (Courtesy C. G. Sloan & Co. Auctioneers. © Peter Harholdt Studio.)*

**Fig. 4–28** *(left) Cameo brooches can make an interesting collection. Cameos similar to these are in current market supply priced from $300. (Collection of Dr. and Mrs. Ben Smith).*

from the workshop of the famous Roman goldsmith Fortunato Pio Castellani (1793–1865). Because of the popularity of the designs of the jewelry uncovered during excavations in Etruscan tombs, Castellani worked to revive the Etruscan technique of gold granulation, along with techniques for micromosaic work (Figs. 4–25, 4–26, 4–27).

Popular brooch materials were coral and ivory, along with cameos carved from hardstone or shell. Shell cameos, popular in the sixteenth century, were revived and glorified in the Victorian period primarily because Victoria herself was fond of the miniature artworks. She gave them away as presents and tried to stimulate a faltering cameo industry in England. Cameos carved in lava originated in the Victorian era. They were carved and sold to tourists on the Grand Tour, who especially wanted souvenirs from Mount Vesuvius. They can be found today and are affordable; they range in price from $100 to several hundred dollars (Figs. 4–28, 4–29).

Classic Victorian brooches feature geometric shapes, abstract designs, or naturalistic arrangements of flowers, birds, and insects. Many have gold ropework or beading,

**Fig. 4–30** *(top left) Black tracery enamel defines this Victorian brooch in an elongated horseshoe motif, $350–$450. (Courtesy C. G. Sloan & Co. Auctioneers. © Peter Harholdt Studio.)*

**Fig. 4–31** *(right) Victorian brooches with black enamel tracery are wearable with today's clothing, and style. Priced from $400. (Courtesy Elizabeth Pierce Green.)*

**Fig. 4–32** *(bottom left) This 18K Victorian bow brooch has lost its black enamel over time, but is still desirable, $125.*

black enamel (Figs. 4–30, 4–31, 4–32), knobs, tassels, or gemstones (Figs. 4–33, 4–34, 4–35, 4–36, 4–37). From a fashion standpoint, the late nineteenth century was notable for wearers of brooches because they were strictly utilitarian items; they held together collars and neck scarfs (Figs. 4–38, 4–39, 4–40). As for jewels in the brooches, there was a move to garnets, rich-red and plentiful from Bohemia.

## GARNET JEWELRY

Pyrope garnets reached their apex of demand during the Victorian era. The collecting of garnets in Bohemia dates back at least to the Middle Ages, when cutting centers were estab-

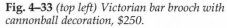

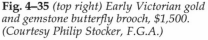

**Fig. 4–33** *(top left) Victorian bar brooch with cannonball decoration, $250.*

**Fig. 4–34** *(top center) Victorian gold and enamel brooch, $300. (Collection of Dr. and Mrs. Ben Smith.)*

**Fig. 4–35** *(top right) Early Victorian gold and gemstone butterfly brooch, $1,500. (Courtesy Philip Stocker, F.G.A.)*

**Fig. 4–36** *(above left) A yellow gold brooch, circa 1870, typical of the sentimental jewelry of the Victorian era, $400. (Courtesy Elizabeth Pierce Green.)*

**Fig. 4–37** *(above right) Sporting themes were popular in both the Victorian and Edwardian eras. Horseshoe motif brooch with turquoise on a knife-edge mounting, $185. (Courtesy P. J. Abramson.)*

**Fig. 4–38** *(third from bottom) Garnet cabochons were called carbuncles when this piece was made about 1870. This brooch has been skillfully restored, $750. (Courtesy P.J. Abramson.)*

**Fig. 4–39** *(second from bottom) One of the most distinctive motifs from the turn of the century is the diamond bar pin. Pictured is a platinum pierced-work pin with diamonds, $650–$850. (Courtesy C. G. Sloan & Co. Auctioneers. © Peter Harholdt Studio.)*

**Fig. 4–40** *(bottom)Sterling was the metal of choice before platinum and white gold. An early-nineteenth-century sterling, marcasite, and pearl brooch, $1,200–$1,500. (Courtesy C. G. Sloan & Co. Auctioneers. © Peter Harholdt Studio.)*

lished in Prague. The garnet-cutting industry reached its zenith in 1780, and Bohemia red garnets were still abundant in Victorian jewelry a hundred years later. Clusters of small brilliant-cut stones have always been the most popular designs (Fig. 4–41).

**Fig. 4–41** *Garnet cluster jewelry is being collected more. Pieces such as these are priced from $350. (Collection of Dr. and Mrs. Ben Smith.)*

The name *garnet* probably came from the Latin word for pomegranate, *granatus*. In the early days of garnet wear, any stone cut in cabochon style was called a carbuncle. Garnets were used as talismans by the Crusaders and soldiers who took them into battle as charms against battle wounds. A rich green variety called demantoid was discovered in Russia in 1868 and reached the peak of its popularity in Art Nouveau jewelry.

Reproduction of old garnet-jewelry pieces are being mass made in Europe today, and collectors should observe the following: Craftsmanship of settings is poorer on the reproductions; faceting of the garnets is poorer; modern garnets are lighter in color; clusters of small stones will be found mounted in three- or four-prong settings as opposed to claw settings in the best genuinely old garnet jewelry. Both genuine antique and reproduction garnet jewelry may be in silver or gold-gilt over silver. Antique gold garnet jewelry will naturally cost more, probably in the $750–$1,000 range, while silver or gold gilt, sometimes called vermeil, goes for $200–$1,000.

# BUTTONS MADE INTO JEWELRY

**Fig. 4–42** *A French cobalt-blue enamel button with a Cupid motif, now a brooch, $650. (Courtesy P. J. Abramson.)*

You may not have given much thought to collecting a piece of jewelry that began its life as a button, but you should. Some of the most beautiful accessories dominating European dress in the early eighteenth century were the French-made gold and jeweled buttons. Buttons were popular in both conventional and flower designs. They were often inlaid with pictures of beautiful women, sporting scenes, flowers, cupids (Fig. 4–42), insects, and erotic subjects. Buttons added to the conspicuous taste for luxury that was prevalent in the mid-eighteenth century: Two to three buttons were needed to fasten a coat at the waist; the rest of the set of buttons were worn to show the costume as a picture gallery. Some buttons even enclosed miniature watches. After the French Revolution, all classes wore simple metal buttons and the French styles and methods were adopted by the English. The English button makers specialized in pewter, silver, brass, and copper, often enameled or embellished with ivory, tortoiseshell, or gems. English-made buttons were made typically in sets of five to thirty-five, cobalt blue was the favorite color in glass or enamel buttons.

Antique buttons can still be found in today's market, frequently with pinstem and "C" clasp added for conversion to a brooch. They are affordable and collectible. Prices range from $100 to $650.

# CHAINS

An assortment of antique chains can form the basis of an unusual and interesting collection (Fig. 4–43). The neck chain is one of the most familiar—as well as useful—items in the antique jewelry world. Chains have historical origins as symbols of office, insignia of various kinds of religious and military orders, and personal ornamentation (Fig. 4–44). Chains have been worn wrapped around necks, wrists, and ankles, and hung with all manner of gemstones, pearls, and other valuable objects.

During the Middle Ages, men and women of rank wore heavy handcrafted twisted links of gold and silver. During the Renaissance, chains were not only part of one's regular costume, but also were used as a mode of currency. It became commonplace to give gifts of gold chains or to use them in payment of a debt. Chains lost their fashion in the seventeenth century but returned to favor in the eighteenth century when they were worn as chatelaines; long chains with dangling implements for household use. In the 1830s, the Albert chain (Fig. 4–45), a long watch chain secured to a buttonhole in the center of a vest, was popular; this type of chain survives today. A chain known as the half-Albert, that hung on only one side of the vest, was also considered stylish. Long chains were also used on muffs, eyeglasses, and lorgnettes (Fig. 4–46). A highly popular chain of the late nineteenth century was known as the Leontine, a short, decorative watch chain named after an actress of the period. It was decorated with tassels of colored gold, and sometimes tassels of silver.

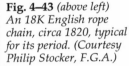

**Fig. 4–43** *(above left) An 18K English rope chain, circa 1820, typical for its period. (Courtesy Philip Stocker, F.G.A.)*

**Fig. 4–44** *(right) A style of chain called a "book chain," because of its flat rectangular-design links. Priced at $1,500 and up.*

**Fig. 4–45** *(center left) The well-dressed Victorian gentleman wore (top) a dress Albert chain, or a half-Albert chain along with a Victorian gold fob. Chains from $350. Fobs from $125 each. (Courtesy of C. G. Sloan & Co. Auctioneers. © Peter Harholdt Studio.)*

**Fig. 4–46** *(bottom left) Late Victorian lorgnettes are highly collectible items. Closed in sterling silver, $350; open in 14K gold, $1,200. (Courtesy Mary Jane Turner)*

# CROSSES

Long before Christianity, the cross was used as an ornamental symbol. It has decorated utensils and vessels, robes and other garments, carpets and banners dedicated to religious uses, and has been used in heraldry and in architecture.

Artifacts and ancient jewelry from India, Syria, Persia, and Egypt show beautiful examples of ornamental crosses. As a religious symbol, the cross in its earliest use was connected with a type of nature worship. Its use as a symbol of Christianity was kept secret until the eighth century.

There are many shapes and styles of crosses. The most common is the Latin cross, in which the upright stem is longer than the crosspiece. When the cross has two crosspieces, it is called a patriarchal cross; with three, a papal cross. A Greek cross has two limbs of equal length; St. Andrew's cross looks like an X; a Tau cross looks like a T; a Celtic cross has a circle in the center. The Maltese cross and the swastika are examples of the more elaborate crosses. Crosses were popular in Europe as peasant jewelry. They can be found in all materials from precious metals to rock crystal.

Fig. 4–47 A turn-of-the-century example of an enameled gold cross in excellent condition, $475. (Courtesy P. J. Abramson.)

The Victorian era abounded in various materials especially for mourning-jewelry crosses, where the bereaved found jet, gutta percha, and bog oak appropriate.

Crosses are one item that antique-jewelry dealers complain are difficult to sell. Therefore, because supply exceeds demand, crosses are relatively inexpensive and can be purchased for only a few dollars to hundred of dollars, depending upon their intrinsic value (Fig. 4–47).

## EARRINGS

We do not know why ancient people wore ear ornaments, but the little history that is known about earrings suggests that putting holes in the earlobes has been practiced since the time of the cave dwellers, probably for sympathetic magic. Early men and women wore earrings as amulets or good-luck talismans. The aboriginal tribes of New Zealand decorated their earrings with teeth from their enemies in order to keep away evil.

In Arab countries, the expression "to have a ring in one's ear" is synonymous with slavery, and there is an ancient Jewish legend that Eve's ears were pierced upon her exile from Eden as a sign of her slavery to Adam. There are many colorful stories about wearing earrings for their magical powers, to secure health, to summon fortune, and to better hear the word of God. What has been established is that different cultures varied in their approach to the question of men and women wearing earrings. In ancient Babylonia, Assyria, and the Orient both sexes wore earrings; in ancient Greece and Rome, only women did.

Earrings were part of therapeutic treatment that stayed on for several centuries. Centuries ago, mothers and midwives perpetuated the custom of piercing the ears of all girls and many boys because wearing earrings was recognized as precautionary treatment of infections of the ears as well as the eyes. Sailors, fishermen, peasants, and artisans wore earrings for the same reasons.

Up until the nineteenth century, few women or girls were without earrings. The techniques of hammering, chasing, casting, engraving, welding, and soldering were all used during the Classical period 500 B.C.–A.D. 500. Many designs have survived over the ages and can be found in specific forms, such as the disk, spiral, boat or crescent-shape, and the disk-and-pendant shape.

All of these earring styles surface in antique and estate jewelry sales. Unless the pair has provenance which documents its origin as truly ancient, be aware that these basic shapes have been reproduced repeatedly throughout the centuries.

The disk—known today as the stud shape—was favored from earliest times and is the most commonly seen design. It is found on the

**Fig. 4–48** *Earrings developed in several basic styles: disk, spiral, crescent, disk-and-pendant and box-shape. Some examples of early Roman earrings, where the various styles and shapes have been mixed. (Courtesy Dover Publishing.)*

women in ancient statues and monuments of Rome and Greece. Unlike the earrings of today, some of the earliest disks had sockets at the back that were fastened by a large stud which fit through the earlobe. This stud not only enlarged the hole in the earlobe, but frequently distended it. The stud fastener has been out of vogue since the post came into use in the mid-nineteenth century.

Spiral-shaped earrings were suspended from a ring through the lobe or were worn like pendants hanging from a stud or disk at the lobe. Spiral earrings of early Greece had ends decorated with animal or human figures much like the

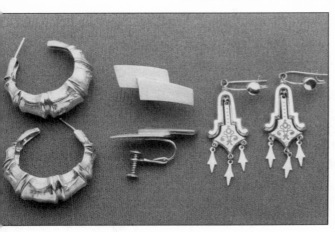

**Fig. 4–49** *A modern adaptation of the crescent style, left. The screw-back finding (center) dates the earrings no earlier than 1900–1910. A pair of black enamel and gold Victorian earrings with earwires, $425.*

popular kissing-ram motifs of the 1980s.

Crescent or boat-shape designs go back to the Bronze Age. Out of fashion in the Hellenistic period, the style later returned as a flattened crescent (Fig. 4–48).

Disk-and-pendant is a sixth-century design that features a disk at the earlobe with one or more pendants attached. The pendant may have been a pyramidal form hung with spirals or often ornamented with chains. This style was revived in the seventeenth century with the *girandole* earrings. The girandole earrings were made with pendants or small, precious stones or pearls (normally three) that were suspended from a main disk at the earlobe. The disk itself could be crescent, bow-swag, horizontal bar, or a combination of all. This popular design has been revived several times and is in use today (Fig. 4–49).

The pendeloque—or pendant—earring evolved from the girandole style in the late seventeenth century. The pendeloque was an excessively long earring that fell to the shoulder.

Victorian earrings reflected the strict codes of social and moral conduct that governed all aspects of daily living. Because fashion in the early nineteenth century called for large, fancy bonnets for ladies and ears that were covered by hair, earrings—when worn at all—were pendant style and generally part of a suite (parure) of matched jewelry pieces reserved for wear with ball dress. From this same time come earrings known as night/day earrings: short for daywear, but with dangling parts that were added to dress them up for the night.

About 1850, earrings became part of daily dress once more; in the 1860s, earrings with drop tassels or gold chains were considered stylish and enjoyed a long reign of popularity.

In her book, *Victorian Jewellery*, Margaret Flower reports how earrings short before 1865 grew so long by 1870 that they began to tangle in bonnet strings; by 1880, small earrings with cabochon-cut stones returned to fashion (Fig. 4–50).

**Fig. 4–50** *Gold and black enamel drop earrings, circa 1865, shows a mixing of motifs with long slender drops, circles and hoops, and cannonball decoration. (Courtesy Lynette Proler Antiques.)*

Just how to circa-date some of the earrings you will find can be an adventure. By observation of the way the earring attaches to the ear, it may be possible for you to make dating decisions. The earliest attachments were the thin wire—either straight or curved—and a stiff wire sometimes referred to as a shepherd's crook. The earliest mention of post backs for pierced ears is provided in an illustration by the German designer Kreuter in 1873. A threaded-post with a nut that screwed onto it was mentioned by French jeweler Eugène Fontenay in the 1880s; and about 1900–1910 the screw-back earring worn without the need of piercing the ear was introduced. The post with a push-on nut was revived in the mid-

1920s, when women were once again demanding earrings for pierced ears.

By 1934 a revolution was at hand in the way earrings were fitted to the earlobe with introduction of the clip. Piercing one's ears had become thought of as a barbaric act, and the clip earring gave women the opportunity to wear ear ornaments without having their ears pierced.

## LOCKETS/PENDANTS

Jewelry that dangles from a chain or ribbon in the form of a locket or pendant has been popular in various eras. Always a convenient way to carry a photograph or miniature painting of a loved one, the classical type of locket is one with a hinged cover which allows either one or two pictures inside.

A pendant or locket is a hanging ornament, usually suspended from a chain or ribbon around the neck but it can also be suspended from a bracelet, earrings, belt, or chatelaine. The origins of the pendant was probably in its wearing as an amulet to ward off evil. During the Middle Ages, pendants had a religious significance that was characterized by the reliquary, a large devotional pendant, or a large enameled or carved cross.

If you collect old pendants or lockets, make a close inspection of the hinge that holds the piece closed: it should be solid and tight fitting. Because of the need for well-fitted hinges, the best lockets were often produced by only the most skilled workmen. In general, only the front and back of the piece will be gold and the rest (inside) may be brass. Most fine old lockets have engraved decoration. Victorian lockets made as mourning jewelry will have black enamel trim and

**Fig. 4–51** *(above left) Mid-Victorian gold pendant with cannetille and cannonball decoration, $450–$650.*

**Fig. 4–52** *(above center) Turn-of-the-century gold, diamond, and opal lavaliere, $1,000–$1,500. (Courtesy Philip Stocker, F.G.A.)*

**Fig. 4–53** *(above right) An early-nineteenth-century pendant with diamonds set in silver and mounted in gold and exhibiting both rose-cut and Old-European-cut diamonds, as well as fine blue sapphires. Price: $1,500. (Courtesy Philip Stocker, F.G.A.)*

**Fig. 4–54** *(right) Art Deco platinum and diamond pendant necklace with old European-cut diamond, surrounded by black onyx and diamonds. The pendant is attached to a platinum chain by collet-set diamonds. Price: $2,500. (Courtesy C. G. Sloan & Co. Auctioneers. © Peter Harholdt Studio.)*

sometimes seed pearls.

Lockets can compose a satisfying collection because they are so wearable with today's garment styles. Among the most affordable of antique jewelry items, lockets and pendants can be purchased for prices ranging from $25 to several hundred dollars. The pendant in Fig. 4–51 is typically Victorian and is priced at $450–$650. Pendants in Figs. 4–52, 4–53 and 4–54 are among the finest examples of their period styles.

**Fig. 4–55** *An Edwardian style festoon necklace. Price: $1,000. (Courtesy C. G. Sloan & Co. Auctioneers. © Peter Harholdt Studio.)*

# NECKLACES

Any jewelry designed to be worn at the neck can be called a necklace. More elaborate forms will include gemstones, and a necklace is included as part of a parure or demi-parure. Many Victorian necklaces were uniquely designed to be dismantled and worn as separate, different ornaments; i.e., a necklace might be fastened at a particular place to become two pieces to be worn as a pair of bracelets.

One of the oldest forms of necklace is called a torque—a twisted collar of precious or base metals found in tombs of northern Europe and Great Britain, especially in Celtic burial sites. The torque may have been a forerunner of the livery collar introduced in the fourteenth century. These collars, worn to declare one's allegiance to the state and monarch, preceded necklaces that were worn to designate membership in various guilds, public office, or order of chivalry.

Early Etruscan necklaces were characterized by exquisite gold work, fretwork and granulation. Necklaces in the Renaissance were large and had jeweled or enameled pendants. Decline in necklace wear in the eighteenth and early nineteenth centuries can be blamed on the cycles of fashion because necklaces regained popularity when apparel became simpler and lighter.

The collector will find a good supply of Etruscan and Egyptian Revival necklaces from the nineteenth and early twentieth centuries, as well as necklaces with naturalistic motifs like pearl flowers, leaves, and drops (Fig. 4–55). These

*Top left: Collectible bracelets from top: Victorian coral bracelet, $500; enamel, pearl and rose-cut diamond bracelet, circa 1860, $5,000; Victorian 18K gold, ruby and bloodstone bracelet, $1,500; gold slide bracelet, $1,500. (Courtesy C. G. Sloan & Co. Auctioneers. © Peter Harholdt Studio.)*

*Top right: Bangle bracelets are among the most enduring styles. Bangles pictured have estimated values of $500–$1,000 each. Victorian cluster garnet jewelry, $200–$1,000. (Courtesy of C. G. Sloan & Co. Auctioneers. © Peter Harholdt Studio.)*

*Bottom right: Typical antique tortoiseshell brooches: star and domed round brooches, circa 1860, $500 each. Rare butterfly tortoiseshell brooch has applied gold instead of inlaid gold. (Courtesy Skinner Inc. Auctioneers & Appraisers, Boston & Bolton, Mass.)*

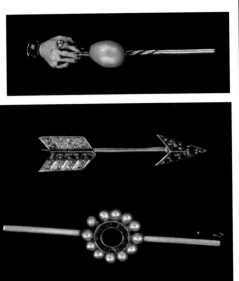

*Top left: Antique white enamel and pearl stickpin hand holding a baroque pearl, $1,450. (Courtesy Skinner Inc. Auctioneers & Appraisers. Boston & Bolton, Mass.)*

*Second from bottom: Two Edwardian gold brooches: arrow jabot accented with twelve demantoid garnets and sixteen rose-cut diamonds; bar pin with sapphires and seed pearls, $250–$350 each. (Courtesy Skinner Inc. Auctioneers & Appraisers. Boston & Bolton, Mass.)*

*Top right: Heart motifs were popular during the romantic Victorian era. This ruby and diamond openwork brooch is typical, $1,500. (Courtesy Philip Stocker, F.G.A.)*

*Bottom left: The heart-with-crown and Scottish thistle were famous Victorian motifs. This brooch is enhanced with seed pearls and amethyst, $2,500. Oval gold, citrine and pearl brooch with inset, $2,500. (Courtesy Lynette Proler Antiques.)*

*Top left: A silver over 18K gold brooch characteristic of the Victorian era styled as a ribbon with rose-cut diamonds and an 11mm baroque pearl, $750. (Courtesy Skinner Inc. Auctioneers & Appraisers. Boston & Bolton, Mass.)*

*Right: An amethyst brooch with textured leaves in 18K gold. English circa 1840, $2,500. (Courtesy Philip Stocker, F.G.A.)*

*Bottom left: A butterfly brooch of the late Victorian period set with old-European cut and old-mine cut diamonds, $3,500. (Courtesy Philip Stocker, F.G.A.)*

Left: A group of antique brooch/pendants: Top right, English miniature portrait on ivory brooch, 15K with diamonds, $1,500; Victorian gold cross pin/pendant with pearls, $700; late seventeenth to eighteenth century English portrait brooch, $2,000; Italian Etruscan revival style micro-mosaic cross pendant, circa 1870, $900; Victorian micro-mosaic dog in gold, amethysts and turquoise, $600. (Courtesy C. G. Sloan & Co. Auctioneers. © Peter Harholdt Studio.)

Right: Representative of the variety of antique and estate items available at auction: earrings in filigree gold, $350; gold and coral brooch, circa 1880, $1,500; Victorian 18K cameo brooch, $1,500; Victorian brooch and earrings with black enamel and pearls, $1,500; cameos in coral, shell and hardstone, $500 each. (Courtesy C. G. Sloan & Co. Auctioneers. © Peter Harholdt Studio.)

Right: Seed pearl jewelry dates from the 1830s. Pictured are 18K gold drop earrings in grape motif with brooch, $1,300; 14K gold and pearl necklace with seed pearls, $1,000; seed pearl portrait pendant, $450; gold, seed pearl brooch, $1,000; and a Georgian gold, enamel and seed pearl pendant with portrait front and back, $3,600. (Courtesy C. G. Sloan & Co. Auctioneers. © Peter Harholdt Studio.)

Left: Victorian gold jewelry: Top, bangle bracelet of a dog wearing a jeweled chain collar, $3,000; two gold and coral cameo bangle bracelets, $500 each; shell and hardstone cameo brooches, $500 each; slides, $150 each. (Courtesy C. G. Sloan & Co. Auctioneers. © Peter Harholdt Studio.)

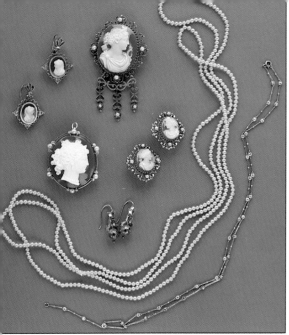

*Upper left: Cameos and pearls are some of the most popular collectibles. Counterclockwise: cameo pendant and earrings, $600; cameo brooch with pearls and diamonds, $700; Victorian cameo earrings, $800; Victorian gold spherical drop earrings, $1,000; seed pearl necklace, $750; diamond collet necklace, $1,500. (Courtesy C. G. Sloan & Co. Auctioneers. © Peter Harholdt Studio.)*

*Upper right: A demi-parure in 18K yellow gold, precious pink topaz and turquoise in its original fitted box, circa 1820. (Photo from the collection of The "Original" Classic International Gem & Jewelry Show, Inc.)*

*Bottom: Georgian 18K yellow gold and precious pink topaz earrings, $2,500; Georgian 18K gold cannetille and turquoise pendant locket with compartment with plaited hair on reverse, $1,500; Victorian gold, ruby and emerald ring, $3,500. (Courtesy Lynette Proler Antiques)*

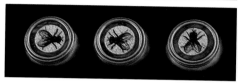

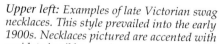

*Upper left: Examples of late Victorian swag necklaces. This style prevailed into the early 1900s. Necklaces pictured are accented with peridots in ribbon and flower motifs, $750 each.(Courtesy Philip Stocker, F.G.A.)*

*Upper right: Victorian 15K yellow gold cross with beaded and wire twist design, accented with small pearls, $550. (Courtesy Skinner Inc. Auctioneers & Appraisers. Boston & Bolton, Mass.)*

*Bottom left: Micro-mosaics were first called "Roman" mosaics. These 18K mid-Victorian micro-mosaic shirt studs have fly designs on malachite, $950. (Courtesy Skinner Inc. Auctioneers & Appraisers. Boston & Bolton, Mass.)*

*Right: Examples of afford-able antique and estate jew-elry: Lapis lazuli silver and diamond cross, $650; turquoise and rose-cut diamond festoon necklace, $1,000; enamel and diamond brooch with earrings, $3,000; Victorian hair memorial brooch, $650; silver gilt gems and seed pearl pendant, $900; silver gilt bracelet in fitted case, $500.(Courtesy C. G. Sloan & Co. Auctioneers. © Peter Harholdt Studio.)*

*Upper left: Art Nouveau platinum diamond and seed pearl pendant (center), $1,600; Edwardian platinum, pearl and diamond pendant, left, $950; right, late Victorian platinum on gold and diamond starburst pin, $650; mabe pearl and diamond ring, $900; double strand of cultured pearls with 18K gold and diamond clasp, $1,000. (Courtesy C. G. Sloan & Co. Auctioneers. © Peter Harholdt Studio.)*

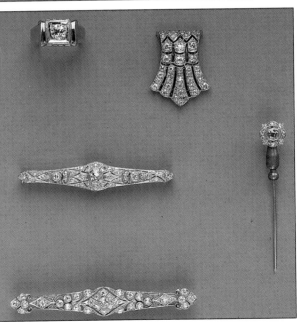

*Left: A man's gold and diamond Retro era ring, $950; 18K white gold, platinum and diamond clip pin, circa 1920, $4,200; Edwardian platinum and diamond bar pin with filigree and old-mine cut diamond, $1,500; platinum and diamond bar pin, $1,800; Edwardian platinum on gold and diamond stickpin, $700. (Courtesy C. G. Sloan & Co. Auctioneers. © Peter Harholdt Studio.)*

**Fig. 4–56** *(left) Late Victorian 14K yellow gold four-strand flexible link choker necklace with center cartouche set with a black onyx cameo; $1,500. (Courtesy C. G. Sloan & Co. Auctioneers. © Peter Harholdt Studio.)*

**Fig. 4–57** *(top right) This Victorian choker for daytime wear has filigree silver and colored-stone ornamentation on a central shield-design clasp. Price: $200. (Courtesy C. G. Sloan & Co. Auctioneers. © Peter Harholdt Studio.)*

**Fig. 4–58** *(right) This transitional amethyst and diamond necklace is a variation of the festoon style. (Courtesy C. G. Sloan & Co. Auctioneers. © Peter Harholdt Studio.)*

are surprisingly affordable at between $1,000 and $2,000. Necklaces in Figs. 4–56, 4–57, and 4–58 display popular Victorian styles.

## RINGS

Of all the types of antique jewelry, the finger ring is the most intimate. It is also the item least likely to have survived the rigors of previous ownership. The shank wears out; two rings worn on the same finger wear each other away. Some old rings cannot be sized because of numerous earlier sizings. The gold can become overworked to the point it falls apart when a torch is put to it (for sizing) and cannot be restored.

In some rings, sizings will alter the size of the internal

radius of the gem setting so drastically that the stone will fall out; the same thing happens when a stone-set ring has been enlarged by soldering a section into the shank. The thick top part may resist the change in radius, and the stones may break or pop out.

One of the most popular rings in the Victorian period—and one of the easiest for buyers to get into a collection—is the "regard" ring, in which the first letter of a series of stones spells out a message, usually "regard" or "dearest." For instance, by using these six stones set in the following order-ruby, emerald, garnet, amethyst, ruby, diamond-the word "regard" is spelled out. Even though the mixed look of the stones may not have been pleasing, it was a popular sentimental gift.

Other rings that speak a language of love are the posy, fede, and giardinetti rings. The posy ring was an early seventeenth- and eighteenth-century love ring usually in a plain gold band with a love poem (called a posy) engraved on the inside. It was often used as a wedding ring in the seventeenth century. The inside poem may be similar to this sweet sentiment: "God hath me sent/My heart's content."

**Fig. 4–59** *A fede—or gimmel ring—was popular as a friendship ring and was sometimes used as a wedding ring.*

A fede (Italian for faith) or gimmel ring, is an eighteenth- and nineteenth-century friendship ring (Fig. 4–59) that was sometimes used as a wedding ring. This design has entwined hoops ending in hands which, when the ring was closed, clasped hands over a heart set on the third and center hoop. In the most elaborate rings, enameled hands closed over a large diamond heart. The Victorian fede rings were sometimes made in one piece (also called Claddagh) and without the

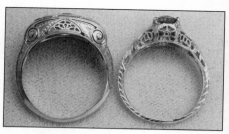

**Fig. 4–60** *(right) Group of Victorian friendship rings spanning the years 1850–1900. Priced $150–$1,000. (Courtesy Philip Stocker, F.G.A.)*

**Fig. 4–61** *(left) Antique ring settings are very important. Pierced and fancy shoulders add interest and value if the piece is in good condition, $350–$450.*

multiple hoops; sometimes the hands had enamel at the wrists to give an impression of cuffs. Gemstone and decorative mountings raise the value of antique rings (Figs. 4–60, 4–61).

The giardinetti ring is typical of the spirit of the eighteenth and early nineteenth centuries. It featured sprays of flowers in precious gemstones; the sprays may be tied with a ribbon or be set in a flowerpot. The baskets are usually in silver with rose diamonds, and tiny flower heads may be set with different-colored gemstones. Affordable diamond and colored stone antique and estate rings like those in Figs. 4–62 and 4–63 are in demand.

Seal or signet rings (Fig. 4–64) have been around since early Mesopotamian times (circa. 3500 B.C.) and were used in both Greece and Rome. In their original use, the signets sealed business deals, inventoried merchant and household goods, and acted as general "lock" on private letters. Georgian and Victorian seals and engraved-stone rings can be found with initials, crests, or coats of arms. Seal rings are plentiful and affordable.

**Fig. 4–62** *(left) A platinum Art Deco ring priced at $850.*

**Fig. 4–63** *(right) A selection of half-hoop Victorian and Edwardian transitional rings priced $700–$1,500. (Courtesy Philip Stocker, F.G.A.)*

**Fig. 4–64** *(center) Seal or signet rings have a history that extends back to Mesopotamia and Egypt. This gold and sapphire seal ring, circa 1885, is typical in that it bears the coat-of-arms of its owner. Early signet and Victorian rings are abundant in the marketplace and priced from $125. (Private collection, Atlanta. Photo by Kathryn Kinev)*

Victorian half-hoop rings with diamonds or combinations of diamonds and colored gemstones, pearls and gemstones, snake designs, buckle designs, crowns-and-hearts designs (Figs. 4–65, 4–66, 4–67, 4–68) are fine collectibles in good supply.

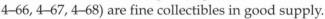

## SCARFPINS AND STICKPINS

Stickpins were born of necessity in the early nineteenth century when men worn cravats, neck scarves that became popular in England and France. To keep cravats fastened, a strong vertical pin, sometimes of silver with a jeweled top was used (Fig. 4–68).

Some of the finest pins from the late nineteenth century are miniature portraits in enamels on gold. Some have the likeness

**Fig. 4–65** *(left) Three Victorian five-stone half-hoop rings, which have desirable carved and pierced settings. The 15K gold rings have diamonds and precious colored gems. Prices start at $1,500. (Courtesy Lynette Proler Antiques.)*

**Fig. 4–66** *(above right) A trio of affordable rings. From left; a Retro white gold, diamond and sapphire ring, $2,250; a contemporary estate ring of platinum, diamond, and pearl, $1,000; and an early-twentieth-century platinum and diamond ring with an old mine-cut diamond in the pierced setting, $600. (Courtesy C. G. Sloan & Co. Auctioneers. © Peter Harholdt Studio.)*

**Fig. 4–67** *(right) Colored gemstone rings are often good buys. Top left, Art Deco-style tourmaline and citrine ring set in platinum, $1,500. Top right, Large citrine ring in a three-color gold setting, $1,000. Bottom left, 14K white gold and aquamarine ring with diamonds. Bottom right, 14K yellow gold, diamond, and sapphire ring. (Courtesy C. G. Sloan & Co. Auctioneers. © Peter Harholdt Studio.)*

of foxes, horses, or dogs; some are set with cameos or gemstones. Stickpins in reverse-crystal intaglio, a technique of carving into the back of a dome of glass and backing with mother-of-pearl, gives the subject a look of three-dimensionality and are highly collectible. Toward the end of the 1800s, women adopted stickpins as scarf pins and sometimes as hatpins.

Some stickpins were made in pairs, joined by a small chain; others will have a "nib," a small metal sheath for the pointed end.

Some scarf pins are fully hallmarked or have karat stamp-

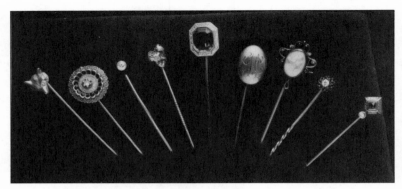

**Fig. 4–68** *Stickpins are collectible and affordable. Pictured are gold, silver, and gold-filled examples that range in price from $10 to $100.*

ing. Pins marked as 9 karat are *later* than 1854, when the 9-karat gold tolerance was introduced into Great Britain.

Special considerations: Hallmarked gold pins are more valuable than those not hallmarked; gold pins are more valuable than other metals; unusual subjects are priced higher than the more commonly found subjects; racehorses are priced higher than dogs. The stickpins will range in price from $25 to $1,000. Reverse-crystal stickpins are elegant, in demand, and affordable—but seldom will be found priced under $1,000.

## WATCH FOBS

Watch fobs, frequently found attached to a chain of the period, are among the most collectible items of nineteenth-century men's jewelry. Fobs and chains were necessary to anchor pocket watches before the wristwatch—invented about 1904 when watchmaker Louis Cartier designed a watch for Brazilian balloonist Alberto Santos-Dumont—became commonplace.

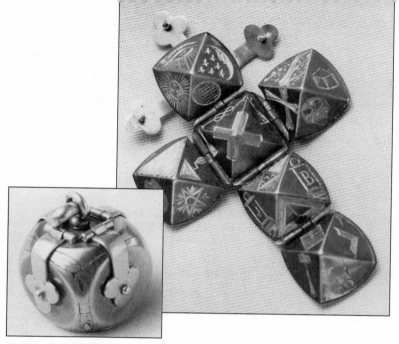

**Fig. 4–69** *(left) The Masonic watch fob comes in a variety of sizes and shapes. The most interesting fobs are the Gold English Masonic balls ranging in size from 11/64 to 1 inch. When opened, the small triangles are engraved with different Masonic symbols.*

**Fig. 4–70** *(right) The Old English square-ball Masonic fob unfolded, dated before 1900. Some new fobs are identical, but their craftsmanship is poor. The four claws on four sides fasten the ball with a small pin on the inside of each claw; new ones are held together with a bottom knob. Prices range from $500–$1,500.*

The watch fobs of the Victorian era, from 1840 to about 1901, are interesting collectibles. Many fobs were made in solid gold, but the majority will be found in gold gilt over base metal, or 9- or 15-karat gold.

Watch fobs are of special interest when set with a fine seal or intaglio. Seals are found in carnelian, bloodstone, onyx and sardonyx. Fraternal insignia (Figs. 4–69, 4–70) and military emblems are particularly collectible.

Fashionable gentlemen also hung other items on their watch chains: penknives, combs, and cigar cutters.

A caveat: When considering old gold chains or fobs, avoid

those with obviously worn spots. Although they can be replated, it may not be worth the money to do so, and some collectors believe that replating an item undermines the integrity of the piece and does not add any value.

## WHAT TO LOOK FOR IN OLD BEADS

Just about any strand of old beads will need restringing because of deterioration of existing cotton or silk thread. If you have your beads restrung, be sure that knots are placed after every bead so that if the strand breaks, you will lose only one or two beads and not the entire strand. Consider replacing an awkward clasp with a comfortable and workable one. Some spring-ring clasps are so tiny and difficult to operate—especially for older women who may have less dexterity in their hands—that they are an exasperating exercise in futility when an attempt is made to wear them.

Some strands of old beads will have a few beads missing; sometimes a collector finds a tiny strand of beads being sold as a bracelet that actually originated as a necklace. If a strand suits your fancy and your pocketbook, but is so short you wonder how it can be worn, have it restrung and add some spacer beads (often gold, silver, or a stone in complimentary color) to get a comfortable, wearable length.

It is sad to see the crude drilling of holes in beads of natural materials. It seems as if the lapidary drilled first from one side, then the other, and left you with a bead with holes that do not meet in the center. This is lamentable because this type of drilling will admit only a tiny string and, when strung, the necklace will not lie properly on your neck. Pass this type of necklace by; you will never be happy with it as part of your collection.

Gem beads have progressed from the crudely shaped native-drilled beads of yesterday; collectors will be able to identify twentieth-century beads by their precision-drilled holes, perfectly round shapes, and high polish. Beads are one of the earliest forms of body ornamentation and were first worn for the magical properties they were supposed to impart to the wearer. This is especially true when the bead was engraved. Favorite materials for antique beads were amber, bone, jet, ivory, agate, lapis lazuli, amethyst, carnelian, turquoise, and glass.

Be aware that not all natural gem beads are of *natural color*. Gem materials have been dyed, heated, and treated by some method or other to enhance their beauty for thousands of years. And be certain that when a dealer calls a strand of old beads "crystal," he or she is not referring to glass, but to rock crystal.

Cloisonné beads are those lovely spheres with brightly colored enamel in strips (cloisons) of metal. This is a very old art form that has been revived and refined century after century. A good sense of touch is needed to detect the old cloisonné beads from the new. Old beads are silky smooth to the touch with no obvious metal projections above the glass enamel portion of the bead. Contemporary and hastily made beads have cloisons that project a fraction of an inch above the enamel. Often the projection cannot be seen easily with the unaided eye, but it can be felt.

Old amethyst, lapis lazuli, and malachite beads may be dulled by time and wear, and can look lifeless. Most beads can be repolished to bring new life to them, but it is a costly project because it is labor intensive. If you simply must have it done, look in the Yellow Pages under Lapidary (or Rock Shop) and look into repolishing (Fig. 4–71).

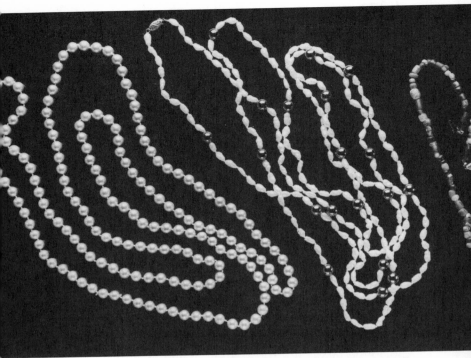

**Fig. 4–71** *Pearl rope, left, and freshwater pearl and hematite bead necklace, center, are examples of what is available in estate goods from $400. The ancient glass bead necklace dated 750–250 B.C., right, is an example of necklaces that may still be found for $350–$450. (Courtesy C. G. Sloan & Co. Auctioneers. © Peter Harholdt Studio.)*

A bitter truth about turquoise beads: Turquoise is a porous stone that usually begins its life as a brilliant blue-green stone. Wear, time, body oil, moisture in the air, and environmental pollutants turn turquoise green. Not a beautiful spring green, but a sickly green that you may find quite unacceptable in a few years. Turquoise requires *care* to keep it beautiful. At this time, there is no known procedure to reverse its aging process or restore the original color. Today's turquoise is often subjected to a wax or acrylic bath to stabilize the material and the color.

# MOURNING JEWELRY

This little-known and misunderstood category of collectible jewelry is said to have begun after the restoration of the British monarchy in 1660 as a form of commemoration of the dead loved one. The custom was never as popular in the rest of Europe as it was in England, so most of the mourning jewelry found in today's marketplace for sale will be of English origin, although the custom was also brought to the American colonies.

In the seventeenth century jewelry called "*memento mori*" ("Remember you must die"), was commonly given to funeral guests of the wealthy deceased. The pieces usually contained inscriptions bearing the name of the departed along with the month, day, and year of death. The jewelry was made in a wide variety of styles, but especially rings and brooches. Sepia paintings of weeping women and willows and urns painted on ivory were popular for surviving spouses. These items usually had a lock of the deceased's hair under a special glass compartment back of the brooch.

Skeletons and skulls were painted under glass or on crystal and set in black-enameled rings. Unmarried women and children were commemorated with white-enameled band rings.

The death of Queen Victoria's consort Prince Albert in 1861 plunged English society into a passionate use of mourning jewelry. There was a return to the custom of braiding hair of the deceased into rings, brooches, bracelets (Fig. 4–72), necklaces, watch fobs or other items of nostalgic jewelry. Some pieces held photographs (Fig. 4–73) as well as locks of hair (Fig. 4–74).

All black and dark materials were popular for use in mourning jewelry. Queen Victoria wore jet buttons (fossilized lignite coal) on black dresses from the time of Prince Albert's

**Fig. 4–72** *(above left) A mid-nineteenth-century gold memorial brooch with braided hair seen in front and a daguerreotype of the deceased on the back. (Courtesy Shirley Sue Swaab.)*

**Fig. 4–73** *(right) The back of the brooch, showing the daguerreotype of the deceased, identified as sixteen-year-old Elizabeth McCune. (Courtesy Shirley Sue Swaab.)*

**Fig. 4–74** *(left) A memorial bracelet, circa 1850. The band is plaited hair; the clasp of woven hair in gold. (Courtesy Shirley Sue Swaab.)*

death until the day she died. The demand for jet from Whitby, England gave rise to an entire industry around the use and export of Whitby jet. This demand for jet led to a deluge of black-glass imitations from Italy and Germany. Onyx was often combined with pearls that represented tears of the grieving survivors. Bog oak and vulcanite were also popular materials.

Mourning jewelry (Fig. 4–75) was produced in a variety of brooches, pendants, rings, bracelets, combs, barrettes, crosses, and beads. Sentimental hearts, arrows, love knots, memorial wreaths, cupids and hands were popular designs.

Collector Shirley Sue Swaab, an expert on mourning jewelry, explains why hair of the deceased was used so prolifically in jewelry by pointing to this advertisement in a mid-nineteenth-century issue *Godey's Lady's Book*:

Hair is at once the most delicate and lasting of our materials and survives us, like love. It is so light, so gentle, so escaping from the idea of death, that with a lock of hair belonging to a child or a friend, we may almost look up to heaven and compare notes with angelic nature—may almost say, "I have a piece of thee here...."

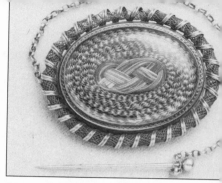

**Fig. 4–75** *This memorial brooch combines the hair of two people, possibly a mother and father. The pin acts as a safety device.*

By the end of the nineteenth century, the passion for hair jewelry had almost faded. It is now being revived by collectors who find the items a charmingly sentimental expression of love. Mourning jewelry in hair or stone is widely available from antique dealers. Because of weak demand, this is an area in which you can make some good buys.

## MILITARY SWEETHEART BADGES

If you are looking for a collectible path to pioneer, investigate sweetheart badges. Military "sweetheart" badges—ornamental badges of European and Early American regiments and battalions—have been ignored, except by devoted collectors of militaria.

Sweethearts (Fig. 4–76) are copies of genuine military regiment or branch insignia that were purchased by soldiers and given to mothers, wives, and girlfriends.

American sweetheart badges go all the way back to the eighteenth century, but not until the Civil War (1860–1865) was there any quantity of badges to be collected. Union Army corps and division badges can be found without much diffi-

**Fig. 4–76** *This sweetheart badge is made from a button of the South Lancashire Regiment. Egypt on the badge comes from the 40th Regiment of Foot. The flank companies were heavily involved in the actions which drove Napoleon from Egypt. Price: $12.50. (Charles A. Edwards, Pass in Review, Grayslake, IL.)*

culty. The firm of Bailey and Kitchen (1832–1846) which became Bailey, Banks & Biddle Company in 1894, were appointed jewelers and manufacturers of insignia of military and naval orders, as well as manufacturers of collar ornaments, rank insignia, and sweetheart badges and regimental coats of arms in gold, gold-gilt, and sterling silver. Many were decorated with enamel, some with gems.

The greatest quantity and most easily obtainable sweethearts, however, are those from Canada, Great Britain, Scotland, and European countries. Europe's long history of armies and battles naturally contributes to richer fields of harvest for this unique jewelry collectible.

British author K. W. Jarmin published a book on military sweetheart brooches in 1981, and suggests collecting them in various categories: (1) any type of different regiments; (2) one type of different regiments; (3) any type of one regiment; (4) infantry of the line; (5) territorial; (6) yeomanry; (7) naval types; (8) RAF types; (9) Colonial and/or Allied forces. Jarmin says that one of the *earliest* British sweethearts is a silver badge dated Birmingham 1889, but he insists they were known and used well before that time, possibly designed and used as a pendant on a neckchain. In general, sweethearts are worn as pins or brooches. Some have safety chains.

The pristine example shown in Fig. 4–77 has a double pin back (Fig. 4–78) which is common if the piece has been fabricated in precious metals, as this one has been. This superb speci-

**Fig. 4–77** *(left)Victorian sweetheart badge in platinum, 18K yellow gold, enamel, and diamonds; fine example of items from this collecting category. The same model is still being made in England by Garrard, the Crown Jewellers of England. This Royal Artillery badge with diamonds, $1,500. (Collection of Ellen J. Epstein.)*

**Fig. 4–78** *(right) Back of the Royal Artillery badge, showing double-pin attachment and fine finish on this article. (Collection of Ellen J. Epstein.)*

men is from the English Royal Artillery and displays a field gun mounted on a scroll with the regimental motto: *Quo Fas Et Gloria Ducunt* ("Wherever Right and Glory Lead"). The badge has the word *Ubique* ("Everywhere") written at the top, indicating that the Royal Artillery has been—and is—present in every engagement of the army. A permanent force of artillery was made part of the British Army establishment in 1716.

The *types* of sweethearts fall into several categories: Pin-bar, badge only, mother-of-pearl disc, mother-of-pearl disc with silver rim, tortoise shell, suspension bar, horseshoes in hollow silver or brass; white enamel background, gold gilt on silver, rifles, swords, whip, bayonet, World War I Western Front trench art.

The pin-bar (Fig. 4–79) sweethearts were the most popular, followed by the badge-only types; they may also be the easiest ones to find and interpret. The suspension badge (suspended from a bar or ribbon) was used mainly during and after World War II. Some brooches can still be found attached to their original sales display card marked "Regimental Badge Brooch," "Regimental Souvenir," "Crest," or

**Fig. 4–79** *The pin-bar sweetheart badges. The sterling silver and enamel sweetheart pictured top is The Royal Armoured Corps from World War I. The badge at bottom is a sterling silver Northampton-shire Regiment badge, bearing the castle and key commemorating its role in the defense of Gibraltar in 1779–1783. Either of these badges can be purchased today for under $20. (Charles A. Edwards, Pass in Review, Grayslake, IL.)*

"Souvenir." However many of the more expensive sweethearts in precious metals and gemstones purchased from jewelry shops are found in presentation cases because they were custom made.

While the serious manufacture of sweethearts declined after World War II, some badges are still being made today by Garrard the Crown Jewellers of England (formerly The Goldsmiths & Silversmiths Company, Ltd., 112 Regent Street, London.) Garrard offers both precious-metal badges and badges set with diamonds and other gemstones. Canadian brooches were also made to high standards, with good detail and enameling (Fig. 4–80).

The collector might assume that the badges are easily placed and dated by hallmarks, but that is not always the case. American sweethearts will probably not be marked with maker's marks. Some English silver brooches have the leopard's head signifying London, the sword and wheat sheaves that indicate the city of Chester (whose assay office closed in 1962), the anchor for the city of Birmingham. A few Scottish badges can be found with the castle hallmark that indicated the city of Edinburgh. Some early English, Scottish, and Canadian badges were assayed and stamped with the maker's initials until 1914. Then, because so many badges were made during World War I, the practice was replaced by simply stamping 9ct, 15ct, sterling, or silver.

How do you value these brooches? Condition affects the price. Damaged enamel or a missing pinstem lowers the value and price. Serious buyers must also investigate other types of military collectibles in order to compare prices of different but related militaria to gauge fluctuating price of sweethearts. When items from any regiment or battalion are in demand, their prices rise; so do their sweetheart badges.

The following British badges are most collectible and thus hard to find:

**Fig. 4–80** *Silver and enamel examples of Canadian sweetheart badges. Priced about $12.50 each. (Charles A. Edwards, Pass in Review, Grayslake, IL.)*

▓ Large Victorian brooches made from 1889–1896 with the makers' initial F.N. and R. & W.

▓ Sweethearts of silver with enameling and marcasites.

▓ Badges with the maker's mark T.L.M.

▓ Horseshoe-type sweethearts *without* the inscription "Good Luck." (This slogan was introduced during World War I. In the era between the two world wars, the horseshoe was reversed from its inverted position to open and upward, and this position was retained on World War II badges.)

▓ Sweethearts with pilot's wings are scarce and highly collectible (Fig. 4–81).

British militaria expert Charles A. Edwards of the company Pass in Review says that some of the most sought-after and collectible sweetheart badges are those of the British and Canadian air corps: "These are generally very beautiful pieces, some with enamels or gemstones, and scarce."

**Fig. 4–81** *Some of the most attractive sweetheart badges are on mother-of-pearl or abalone shell. Among the most difficult to find are sweethearts from the Royal Flying Corps, bottom right. The badge is that of the pilot's wing, a replica of the one worn on the tunic, over the heart. The motto, then and now, is Per ardua ad astra which means "Through difficulties to the skies." The badges are priced at $50 each. (Courtesy Steve Johnson.)*

According to Edwards, the collector lucky enough to find a British pilot's sweetheart wing badge will pay up to $300 for a fine example.

Many naval badges are also rare. The silver Submarine Service badges exist but are difficult to find. The silver and enamel "Her Majesty's Yacht *Britannia*" bar-pin badge is also scarce.

Trench badges refer to sweethearts made by soldiers in their spare time from war scrap; i.e., metal from a crashed or damaged aircraft, spent bullet casings, and so forth.

Brooches depicting well-known battlegrounds of World War I are collectible trench art. These items were made by British, Allied, and German soldiers as gifts. Most names of the battlegrounds have long been forgotten, but badges from the Western Front signed Somme, Bapaume, Arras, Amiens, or The Balkans are sought after.

Where do you go to collect these? Military shows and military weapons shows. These specialty events travel all over the United States, with dealer caravans putting on weekend sell-and-trade fairs in hotels and motels. These are your primary hunting grounds where you can find dealers who specialize in sweetheart badges. If you have an interest in British, Canadian, or Scottish badges, Charles Edwards at

Pass in Review can help. Contact him at P.O. Box 622, Grayslake, IL 60030.

## PROPAGANDA JEWELRY

Closely associated with military jewelry and sweetheart badges is propaganda jewelry, sometimes called political jewelry. It consists of badges, brooches, and pendants originally designed and sold to promote some cause, usually political. The practice began first in Europe, where the ruling powers had been in conflict for hundreds of years.

**Fig. 4–82** *A propaganda-jewelry brooch with the French cock trampling a German eagle, circa 1870. Yellow gold, $350. (Courtesy P. J. Abramson.)*

Some political jewelry takes the form of an animal and often needs to be studied carefully to understand the hidden message. Animals were used to symbolize nations, and their images were fixed by the mid-1700s; they are still in use today.

Generally, these symbols stuck with the country and can be seen repeated often in satirical political prints (cartoons) that flourished in the eighteenth century. France was represented by a cock (Fig. 4–82); a dog was the symbol for Genoa; England was a lion. However, around 1780, when depicted individually, both Holland and England were symbolized as lions; sometimes when both appeared in the same cartoon

Holland remained a lion and England was depicted as a leopard. Austria was symbolized as the eagle, Spain a leopard, Prussia a wolf; later, Holland was also depicted as a boar.

When these animals are found on jewelry pins and brooches of the eighteenth century, the chances are high that they were made with deep political meaning and represent more than pure ornamentation. They are affordable and range in price from $25 to over $500, depending upon their material.

## CHAPTER FIVE

# COLLECTING CYCLES AND STYLE REVIVALS

## TRENDS, FADS, FASHIONS

A *trend* is a current style or fashion preference by consumers, such as the current trend toward estate and antique jewelry as both fashion statement and long-term investment.

A *fad* may be looked upon as something of immediate fancy in the market. *Webster's Dictionary* describes a fad as "A practice or interest followed for a time with exaggerated zeal." A fad can be likened to a comet zooming across the sky—of immediate interest, but suddenly vanishing—like the mood ring of the 1960s, and the pet rock of the 1970s.

Fads have been around for centuries; for example, there was a fascinating jewelry fad that took place at the end of the nineteenth century when some women wore jewels as nipple ornaments. Little documentation on this subject has been found, but it has been mentioned in the writings of the distinguished contemporary English physician-author Dr. John

Grant. He writes that some women at the turn of the century had their nipples pierced like earlobes. Gold rings, some with diamonds or rubies, were inserted through the nipple and hung from the areola. If this fad sounds painful, it most probably was, and the pain could have been the reason why nipple jewelry did not last very long.

A fad can be something like a fake-pearl choker, especially when it is made by Kenneth Jay Lane and its constant wearer is someone as conspicuous as Barbara Bush. Lane, a noted jewelry designer, feels that the former First Lady's penchant for costume jewelry greatly influenced the public; it put his fake pearls in a category of much-sought-after adornment. In a meeting, the designer told a crowd not to refer to his costume jewelry as junk. "I prefer to call in junque," he said. "It brings the price up that way."

A *fashion* on the other hand can be of short- or long-term duration and is influenced primarily by the surrounding cultural, political, and social climate.

In the 1820s, there was a fashion called the *ferronnière*, a band with a jewel in the middle that was worn around the forehead. It appears in many old European paintings. Due to political, social, and cultural changes, this was a shortlived fashion. Yet the fashion for the solitaire diamond ring that became popular in the 1880s remains to this day, regardless of wars and sweeping changes of social and political orders.

## FUTURE TRENDS— THE NEW ANTIQUES

Who is setting the trends today? The professional woman. With disposable income, political and social liberation, and the chance to plan her own future, many professional women today do not wait for someone to give them jewelry, or to inherit grandmother's treasures. Today they buy their own jewelry, and wear it regularly. As contemporary jewelry becomes tomorrow's antiques, so more modern jewelry is being fabricated with specific style and design, good clasps, and in precious metals and gemstones. The nineties professional woman believes that items grow more valuable when they are made in precious materials.

What kind of jewelry constitutes the new antiques of the future? According to a recent survey, the most popular gold jewelry items are neck chains, earrings, charms, bracelets, and rings in that descending order. Gold wedding rings, earrings, chains, and charms are worn by people in all levels of society throughout the world. Those most likely to become antiques of the future are the ones that are most precious today. At last, designers are waking up to the fact that a piece of jewelry should not be just for a sale, but for life.

## IMPORTANT DESIGNER NAMES AND MANUFACTURER'S MARKS

Ask anyone to name an important manufacturer or designer of antique jewelry, and chances are 90 percent will say "Tiffany" or "Cartier." They should not forget Fabergé, one of the most important nineteenth and twentieth century designers.

The Fabergé family settled in St. Petersburg, Russia, in 1842, where Gustave Fabergé, the father of the more famous Carl, set up a jewelry business. Carl was sent to Germany and France to learn his trade, and at twenty-four took over the family business. The firm was assured of world fame because of patronage by the czars and nobility of Russia, the British royal family, the crowned heads of Europe, and the shah of

Persia. The house of Fabergé was confiscated by the Bolsheviks in 1918 after the Soviet revolution.

Fabergé reached the pinnacle of his reputation with his exhibition in Paris at the 1900 World Fair—Exposition Internationale Universelle—and was awarded the *Légion d'Honneur* for his marvels. The Paris exhibition produced an international reputation for Fabergé and earned him support from royalty and the aristocracy of Europe, India, and the Orient. By 1898 more than 700 craftsmen worked in the Fabergé factories in St. Petersburg, Moscow, Kiev, Odessa, and London. Every piece that left his workshops was marked with his individualized signature. There is a great deal of reproduction Fabergé jewelry on the market today. However, a giveaway that all may not be correct is that the Fabergé name may be spelled out in English characters instead of the correct cyrillic lettering (Fig. 5–1). In addition, the Fabergé name or initials were often combined with the initials of the workmaster who actually made the piece. If, for instance, you see the letters KØ H.W. inside a mounting, it stands for Fabergé's master Henrik Wigstrom (H.W.). There were many workmasters, but not all made jewelry. There are many books about Fabergé that give complete listings of workmasters and jewelry marks. Consult your library.

**Fig. 5–1** *The Fabergé signature in Cyrillic lettering.*

Some other important European jewelers' and manufacturers' names of the late nineteenth century are R. & S. Garrard, Hancocks & Co., Charles Ashbee, Asprey & Co., and Cartier in Paris. Among American jewelers and manufacturers are Bailey, Banks & Biddle; Black, Starr & Frost; J. E. Caldwell, and Peacock & Company.

# HOW TO RECOGNIZE METALS AND MANUFACTURING METHODS

Although it is not necessary to become a bench jeweler to be knowledgeable about manufacturing methods, it is necessary to be able to distinguish between those pieces that are machine made and handmade. Just a little study and practice will go a long way toward minimizing mistakes in buying. Handmade antique jewelry should be more expensive than

**Fig. 5–2** *This ring shank illustrates porosity.*

machine-produced antique jewelry, but that higher price *must* also be justified by superior craftsmanship and condition, not just because it is old. Although some poor handmade jewelry exists, your mission as buyer is first to be able to distinguish the handmade from machine made.

The types of manufacturing are handmade, cast, machine or die-stamped. And there can be combinations of all of these. Typical indications of handmade jewelry are overlapping and often incomplete cuts that do not join other parts of the design, and tool marks.

The clue in identifying cast jewelry is the visible signs of porosity (Fig. 5–2)—tiny pits or bubbles on the underside of the mounting. These are the result of hastily cast articles and the unsuccessful burnout of what is called the lost wax process of jewelry manufacture. Porosity also occurs sometimes even if the undersides have been hand finished. Cast manufacture can also be determined by burrs (rough or unfinished portions) on the jewelry.

**Fig. 5–3** *An example of the die-striking method of manufacture.*

The third method most frequently used is stamping or die striking (Fig. 5–3). As early as 1852, the machinery for die-struck articles was being used in Paris. Die-struck pieces can sometimes be identified by the bright finish on their underside and in some tiny areas of the mounting. The edges on some die-struck jewelry articles often have a knife-edge appearance.

### METALS

Being able to identify various metals is a challenge, sometimes even to the experts. In 1732, Christopher Pinchbeck, an English watchmaker, invented a metal imitating gold by alloying copper and zinc. The new metal was used in England for imitation-gold jewelry and watchcases. Other imitations were developed, so other types of gold metals of a later period are frequently referred to as pinchbeck. The secret of the original pinchbeck metal died with its inventor.

During Queen Victoria's reign new materials and techniques were introduced into the jeweler's craft. Most significant was the electroplating process first used by the firm of Elkinton and Wright about 1840. Until the discovery of this process, cheaper jewelry had been made using the pinchbeck imitation-gold process. The advantage of electroplating was that the entire surface of a piece in base metal could be covered with real gold and looked indistinguishable from a genuine solid gold piece of jewelry. The marks EPNS, EPBM, EPWM, and EPC all mean the item has been electroplated.

Jewelry marked "GF" or "gold-filled" is not made of solid gold, but refers to jewelry made from layers of 10- to 14-karat gold that are bonded to the surfaces of other metals. The term "gold filled" is uniquely American and dates from about 1870.

It is common to find gold jewelry without any markings whatsoever, *especially that made during the Victorian period*. When trying to distinguish base metal, look for telltale dark spots in areas that are subject to normal wear; these may indicate base metal. Also, sniff or "taste" for the smell of copper or brass. Base metal is discerned by its metallic smell and taste, especially when warmed by rubbing in one's hand.

If a piece is white gold, it is unlikely to be an antique because white gold was developed about 1910. This metal is an alloy of gold with a high percentage of silver or other white metal. Harold Newman's *Illustrated Dictionary of Jewelry* defines white gold as a term that was also applied to the ancient metal called electrum.

Platinum was used for jewelry as early as 1828, but not in great quantity until after 1890. The metal is strongly associated with jewelry of the Edwardian era.

Most people realize that sterling-silver jewelry has a higher intrinsic material value than other grades of silver, but not everyone can recognize sterling. The simplest way to identify sterling silver is by searching for the marking on the item. The decimal marking .925 indicates sterling silver. Coin silver, which is 90 percent pure silver, is written as .900. The term nickel—or German—silver, refers to an alloy of copper, zinc, and nickel and does not contain any genuine silver.

Colonial jewelry makers fashioned items by using techniques learned during lengthy apprenticeships. Since early America produced no raw silver or gold, craftsmen relied upon coins and other miscellaneous pieces of metal as raw material. No law or metal standard existed in the American colonies, so the pledge of quality of an item was trust in the craftsman who backed the jewelry with his reputation.

## HALLMARKS

The assay and stamping of silver was instituted in England in 1300 by a statute of Edward I; thus it is the oldest form of quality control still in use in the world. Generally the hallmark has four component punch marks, and they give the following information: maker's mark, type of metal used in the piece and standard of its purity, identity of the assay office; year in which the item was assayed. A maker's mark is the initials of the goldsmith or manufacturer who actually did the work, but, in a small number of cases it may be the mark of the retailer who sold the piece. In England, the maker's mark is registered with an assay office.

**Fig. 5–4** *The lion marks an item as British sterling- silver.*

English sterling silver is indicated by a lion (Fig. 5–4) but there are no numbers to show that it is sterling. Since 1798, two hallmark standards have been recognized for gold in Great Britain, the 18 and 22 karat marks. In 1854, lower standards of 9, 12 and 15 karats were introduced; in 1932, the 12K and 15K were dropped and replaced by the 14K standard. The following table will help you recognize English standards for gold marks (Fig. 5–5). In the assay marks before 1975, the crown was used only on the higher (18 and 22K) gold contents. Some marks show the gold both as a karat number (parts per 24) and as a decimal.

The *assay mark*—or town mark—indicates where the piece was assayed, and will be one of the following cities: London, Birmingham, Edinburgh, Sheffield, Dublin, Chester, Glasgow, Newcastle, and Exeter. This town mark gives clues to the area in which a manufacturer worked, but cannot be relied upon totally as some manufacturers worked in one town but sent their items to another for assay.

The *year mark* is indicated by a letter of the alphabet that was different for each assay office and changed at various times of the year depending upon which office was doing the marking.

The use of the *sovereign's head* in assay marks between 1784 and 1890 means that duty was paid on the item. After 1867, imported goods received the mark "F" in addition to the normal marks.

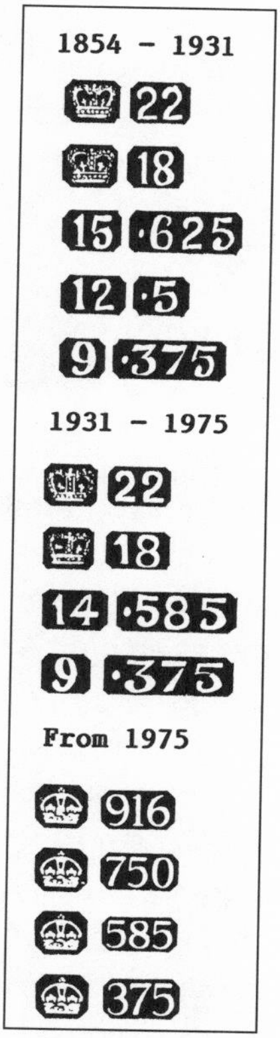

World events have meant great social and economic changes in the former Soviet Union. Consequently, Russian antiques—including jewelry—will certainly be highly collectible in the coming years. If you are interested in building a collection, now is an excellent time to begin; but first learn about Russian metal standards.

**Fig. 5–5** *Marks used for standards of gold on British items assayed after 1854.*

Russian silver jewelry should be examined closely. It does not have the same purity of content as Western silver, and the standards are not described in ounces, karats, or grams, but in zolotniks, a Russian measurement of weight. Ninety-six zolotniks equal one Russian pound. The numbers of silver are described as 84, 88 (below U.S. sterling silver standard) and 91, above our sterling standard. Gold is described by the numerals 56 (14K), 72 (18K), and 92 (23K). Platinum has received no hallmarks. The Russian marks for year and town will also be found on most jewelry objects.

## MORE ABOUT COLORED GEMSTONES

There are imitation and synthetic gemstones found in estate and antique jewelry, along with the natural-colored stones. It will be of benefit to buyer and collectors to understand which gems *should* be found in a piece of jewelry, and enable one to recognize anomalies in what is purported to be an antique.

Gemstones that "belong" in old jewelry are many:

*Amber* is the million-year-old fossilized resin from now-extinct coniferous juniper trees. When the resin was still fluid, it would attract passing insects and floating plantlife, once the resin hardened, the "visitors" would be trapped and remained imprisoned in it forever. Today such bits of prehistory are considered most valuable, and a chunk of amber with fossil inclusions carries a higher price than clear amber of similar size. However, like all natural gemstones, amber is widely imitated, and some ingenious fakes with whole or parts of insects, fish scales, and leaves are on the market. Usually a transparent gemstone, amber ranges in color from pale yellow to orange and all shades of brown and red, as well as gray and bluish. The best material is from the Baltic coasts of Denmark, Poland, and Germany, but amber also comes from Sicily, Romania, the Dominican Republic, and Africa. The dark red amber, often found in antique beads, is the most sought-after and expensive.

*Agate*—Much Victorian jewelry was set with moss agate,

a stone that looks as if it has little branches or trees inside. Agates are cut in cabochon form; they are hard and wear well.

*Bloodstone* is a member of the chalcedony (quartz) family. It is an opaque dark-green stone with red spots. Many pieces of antique jewelry are set with it, particularly men's rings. Some fine bloodstone cameos were produced in the nineteenth century, with the red spots pointing up the cleverness of the artisan. The stone will be either cut in cabochon or with a flat top.

*Carnelian*—This brownish-red stone of the chalcedony family is often found in antique jewelry, sometimes cut in cabochon and frequently as beads. Some carnelian material is quite translucent and provides fine carving material for intaglios. Relating its color to sympathetic magic, the stone has a history wrapped in superstition as a gem that would stop bleeding if placed on a wound.

*Coral*—A very popular material for beads in the Victorian era with colors ranging from white to orange-red to a deep red called oxblood. In old paintings, many babies and young children were pictured wearing coral necklaces to protect them from danger and disease. Coral pacifiers were also popular during the Victorian age.

The most desirable shades of coral are salmon-pink, dark red and angel-skin. Quality is defined by lack of pits or holes in the material.

*Diamonds* have been known for many centuries; they were mentioned in India as early as 800 B.C. They were carried by traders to Greece and Rome in the west and China in the east, where the primitive artisans and craftsmen found the substance so hard that they could not work it easily. It was centuries later before the technique of using diamonds to cut and polish diamonds arose.

In the early days of diamond use, the diamond crystal in

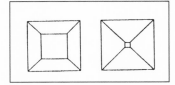

**Fig. 5–6** *The table-cut style*

its natural octahedral shape was used in all jewelry where diamonds were set. The octahedral—or eight-sided—form, resembled two pyramids joined at their bases. The normal setting showed only the top portion of the crystal; and the lower part of the pyramid was hidden. Decades later, the tips of the crystals were removed, creating what is called a table-cut stone (Fig. 5–6). Then, in the fifteenth century, Louis de Berquen of Belgium is reported to have invented the first polishing wheel. It used a compound of diamond dust and oil to create facets on diamonds; Berquen called this style a rose-cut. The rose-cut diamond comes in four forms: Holland rose with 24 facets; half-Holland-cut with 18–20 facets; Antwerp-cut with 6–8 facets; and a 3–facet cut (Fig. 5–7).

In the early seventeenth century, the Mazarin cut was developed and named in honor of the famous French cardinal. In this cut, diamonds had 17 facets both top and bottom. The Mazarin was a revolutionary cut because it allowed more light into the diamond. It was not until about 1700 that the

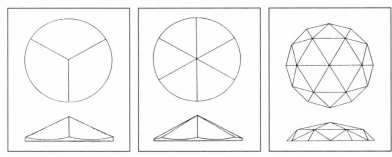

**Fig. 5–7** *Three forms of cutting the rose-cut. Left to right: Three-facet rose-cut; six-facet (Antwerp-cut) style, and full 24-facet Holland rose-cut.*

Venetian Vincenzo Peruzzi created the brilliant cut with 56–58 facets, the forerunner of the brilliant cuts used today.

Diamond cuts are important in antique jewelry in helping you circa-date. Up until about 1920, the rose-cuts, old-mine-cut and old-European-cut styles were found most frequently.

While the identity of the first man to wear diamonds is not known, the first woman reported to have worn diamonds, in an attempt to attract attention to herself, was a beauty of the French court Agnès Sorel, in the year 1444. Mme. Sorel was in love with King Charles VII (the same monarch for whom Joan of Arc had fought and died), and she was desperately trying to catch the royal eye. She chose to wear diamonds in a shocking attempt to stand apart from the other court beauties. History records that Agnès borrowed diamonds from the men in her family and had them made into a necklace. Her bold actions not only got her noticed by the king, but she became the royal mistress.

Since earliest times, diamonds have been believed to possess protective powers. Napoleon I had a diamond set in the hilt of his sword, confident that it would protect him in battle and secure victory. Napoleon III wore a lucky diamond ring that had belonged to Napoleon I. It is reported to have been buried with him. Diamonds were extremely popular in the 1850s, and a vast new discovery of diamond deposits in South Africa increased the supply needed to fill a growing demand.

*Emeralds*—The emerald was first offered for sale in 4000 B.C. in Babylon, the earliest-known gem market.

From the beginning of history, there have been only two sources for the finest emeralds: the Egyptian mines that once belonged to Cleopatra, and the Colombian mines of South America. Catherine the Great of Russia also had emeralds that were supposed to have been obtained from mines in the

Ural Mountains. A collection of them was sold in the early twentieth century for more than three-quarters of a million dollars.

Most emeralds are characterized by vast networks of cracks, lines and spots inside the stones. The French call this the "*jardin*," (garden), and occasionally American jewelers use that terminology. It is a lovely way to romance the stone and sounds better to the customer than "cracks, lines, veils or undissolved mineral spots."

Emeralds range in color from very pale green to a deep greenish-blue color. Most of the value of an emerald is in the color, the preferred color is a deep, clean vibrant green without dark overtones.

*Goldstone*—This cabochon-cut stone is not natural. It's a man-made brownish-red material that looks as if it contains many tiny gold flakes. The imitation stone was developed around 1840, and the process of manufacture involves addition of copper filings to glass. Goldstone imitates the natural gem sunstone.

Goldstone looks good and wear well. It is found in many pieces of antique jewelry, especially women's rings.

*Jet*—This form of fossilized lignite coal was abundant in England around 1800 (see Mourning jewelry). Jet jewelry is still found abundantly at antique-jewelry shows and is affordable.

*Moonstone*—This gemstone, always cut in cabochon, was popular during the late Victorian and Art Nouveau eras. The stone has a colorless and slightly cloudy look, with brownish to bluish overtones. Moonstones are also found carved and set in rings or strung in necklaces. This stone exhibits a billowy sheen that moves across the face of the stone.

*Opal*—Large deposits of opal were discovered in Australia in 1849, and it has been a popular stone since that time. Before the Australian deposits were discovered, most opals came from Hungarian mines, then from Mexico.

The Empress Josephine owned an opal that she called "The Burning of Troy" because of its display of red and orange colors. Other colors displayed in opals are greens, blues, yellows, and black. Because opal material dries out easily, it develops cracks that are unsightly. Inspect opals in antique jewelry carefully to be assured they are in good condition. Once the cracks develop, they are worthless.

*Pearls*—Natural pearls have been coveted since ancient times, and the best pearls used to come from the Persian Gulf. The pearls found in antique jewelry today and called "Oriental" pearls by their seller would have been part of the bounty of the Persian Gulf.

When cultured pearls came onto the market about 1910, it signaled a demise for natural pearls. Cultured pearls were cheaper, quality control could be maintained, and the public couldn't tell the difference.

The only viable test for separating natural from cultured pearls to this day is by X-ray analysis. However, this costly procedure is necessary only when the price of jewelry spirals upward so dramatically, because the pearls are being sold as natural, that the buyer must have certification and guarantee of their origin.

In most instances, the only real identification needed is separating imitation from cultured pearls. This can be easily accomplished with the tooth test. While this may not look hygienic or aesthetic, it works. Gently rub the surface of a pearl (that you are testing) across the edge of an upper or lower tooth; you can feel a certain grittiness in a cultured pearl. If, however, the material feels smooth or slick without any hint of grit, it is probably plastic or glass. This technique should be practiced at home with a strand of imitation pearls and a strand of cultured pearls until the "feel" or observation of difference is understood completely (Fig. 5–8).

*Quartz-Amethyst*—The purple variety of quartz (rock

**Fig. 5–8** *Pictured center is a carved red coral cameo, seed pearl and fresh water pearl multi-strand bracelet, $300–$400. While this is typically Victorian, many pearl reproduction-antique-jewelry items are flooding the market. The single-strand pearl necklace, right, was identified by the GIA as natural pearls (not cultured). The only accurate method currently used to separate natural from cultured pearls is by X-ray analysis. (Courtesy C. G. Sloan & Co. Auctioneers. © Peter Harholdt Studio.)*

crystal) is called amethyst. This stone was originally imported into Greece from Persia. The ancients believed that the amethyst could be used against drunkenness: Wine drunk from an amethyst bowl would not cause intoxication! This belief persisted for centuries.

You can use a simple field test to separate amethyst quartz from glass. Touch or lightly rest the unidentified item on your cheek: quartz has high thermal conductivity and will feel cool to the touch; glass, on the other hand, will usually feel warm.

*Ruby*—Among the most precious of all gems, it is known that both rubies and sapphires first appeared in Europe during Greco-Roman times. They are found mainly in Myanmar (formerly Burma), Thailand, and Sri Lanka in a wide range of colors from pale pink to deep purplish-red.

The deep red of the ruby convinced the ancients that the gem had hidden powers; they called it "the stone of life." The ruby was also believed to work cures for illness, and worn into battle was said to make one invincible. In finest qualities rubies are the most expensive of gems and can be more expensive than diamonds of comparable quality and carat weight.

Along with carat size, intensity of color is the key to value. A tiny pale pinkish ruby sells for a few dollars for the stone, while an intense bright-red stone of five-to-ten carats is worth thousands of dollars per carat.

*Sapphire*—Cousin of the ruby, chemically both gems consist of corundum. Sapphires come from Thailand, Sri Lanka, India, Australia and the state of Montana. The Kashmir stones with a characteristic "cornflower" blue color are the most highly prized.

The sapphire has been called the gem of wisdom and has always been a coveted gemstone. Like the ruby, the key to its value lies in intense color saturation, flawlessness of the stone, and carat weight.

*Topaz*—This yellowish-brown to pinkish-mauve stone is usually transparent and faceted. It was popular between 1810 and 1830 and was worn in necklaces by those who could not afford diamonds. Russian pink topaz is a highly collectible gem; keep a special lookout for it.

# OLD GLASS (PASTE) IS NICE

The eighteenth century was the age of paste. At that time there was no special social stigma attached to the wearing of glass imitation stones, in fact quite the contrary. Glass—or paste—was worn by both those who could well afford genuine gemstones, and by those who could not.

In 1724, a lead glass that is often referred to as *strass*, was invented by George Strasser of Strasbourg, while he worked as a jeweler in Paris. The disdain that most collectors feel today for paste jewelry is a modern attitude and was not shared by people of the eighteenth century who preferred to wear paste jewels especially when traveling because of the fear of highwaymen and the dangers of robbery. But the glass jewels of the eighteenth century were different from the glass jewels of today and that may account for some of the acceptance of the early paste. In the eighteenth century, the glass jewels were well designed and were made as carefully as precious stones. The French were especially careful to set blue-paste cabochon stones that rivaled their natural sapphire counterparts in beauty and appeal. A special type of paste—opal glass—was developed in the eighteenth century: it consisted of translucent pink glass set over rose-colored foil and was enormously popular.

The best examples of glass were made before 1820. After 1850 jewelry styles changed, and the use of paste was directed almost entirely toward imitating diamonds. Later, glass jewels ceased to be coveted objects and their popularity plunged dramatically.

Collectors need to be aware that paste stones have a tendency to wear at the facet edges and abrade heavily, so they are not very likely to deceive you as a buyer. The antique-paste items made by skilled craftsmen have a collectible value of their own, and good examples are pricey.

Make the following tests to separate glass from stone: Take the gem's temperature by touching it to your lips or with your tongue. Glass has no crystal structure and will remain warm to the touch; mineral-based crystal will stay cool. Examine the stone with your 10X loupe and look for such indicators of glass as doughnut shaped inclusions, round bubbles, molded (as if poured) facets or cabochons, and conchoidal (concentric) chips.

## CHAPTER SIX

# $W$HERE THE $A$NTIQUE $J$EWELRY $I$S $F$OUND

## TO MARKET, TO MARKET

The pleasures of buying antique jewelry go well beyond the enjoyment of finding body ornamentation; there is the added thrill of a treasure hunt. There are several sources—or markets—where this elusive quarry can be found, the most obvious being the local antique dealer's shop, a retail jeweler with a well-stocked showcase of estate goods, crafts fairs, private individuals, and mom-and-pop stores—especially if they advertise that they buy old gold and old jewelry.

Still, the hunter must go beyond these traditional outlets and think creatively, scouting museum shops, specialty kiosks, stores in antique arcades, traveling antique shows—especially charity-oriented ones—and court- and government-ordered auctions.

Many better department stores go into estate-jewelry sales themselves; others lease space to outsiders. Leasors often circulate estate goods among several leased departments in various cities, assuring customers of a wide variety of choice.

That was a market overview. Here are several of the more obscure markets:

Consider pawnshops. Legitimate pawnshops serve a real purpose in the community and help people pressed for cash with short-term loans. If, however, the loan is defaulted on, the jewelry (often antique) is sold by the owner/operator of the business, and can result in some bargains for the savvy jewelry buyer.

Traveling gem and jewelry shows, gem and mineral shows, specialty collectors shows like military, paper, doll, glass, coin and stamp are often rich hunting grounds overlooked by the jewelry buyer.

There are finds to be made at the specialty sales held by local historical societies such as the Daughters of the American Revolution (DAR), Daughters of the British Empire, Colonial Dames, and many others. Look for advertisements from small local dealers who participate in regional shows sponsored by women's clubs, church groups, or charities. Another hidden hunting ground may be the resale shop of a local institution such as a hospital. One Colorado woman gemologist who runs the gift resale shop for a hospital/nursing home reports that she handles a large quantity of estate and antique jewelry. You can find out about these outlets from various organization and club newsletters or by consulting your Yellow Pages under "jewelry—antique."

Banks auction off the contents of safety-deposit boxes when the box has been abandoned and the boxholder cannot be located. One of the best hunting grounds for old jewelry is found at police-department auctions. Some police departments let their confiscated and unclaimed merchandise pile up for years before they auction it off; they literally do not know the value of what they have and rely on the auctioneer who has bid for the job.

Kay Peters of Houston purchased ten strands of fine quality cultured pearls at a police auction in the mid-1980s for fifty cents per strand, and a marcasite pin for a few dollars. Later she learned from an appraiser that the pin was a valuable antique and that the pearls were worth hundreds of dollars per strand.

There is hardly a city in the United States today that does not have an antiques arcade or mall of some kind. While some of them cater only to furniture or other specialities, the wise collector knows that *all* antique dealers come across items they don't normally sell and put away in a box or drawer; these goods are known in the trade as "sleepers." The hunter should always inquire about any "old jewelry" that the dealer might have. You can never tell just what could turn up! Remember, general-antiques dealers usually keep this kind of hoard out of sight.

There is a market for collectors that can be referred to only as a tertiary market. If a collectible is very specialized—for example, Hummel figurines or Bradford plates—people often band together and form a club especially for that object. The advantage of participation in such groups is twofold: You not only net special expertise from fellow collectors, but you also can gain access to buyers and sellers not otherwise obtainable. Two such markets we know about for jewelry buyers are The Bead Society of Greater Washington, P.O. Box 70036, Washington, DC 20088–0036, if you love beads and the Cameo Collectors Society, 496 Chenango Street, Binghamton, NY 13901, if cameos interest you.

# STALKING THE ANTIQUE
## JEWELRY SHOW

In pursuing antiques, it costs money to make the hunt. It is one thing to combine taking in an antiques show while driving about on business, but to go out deliberately to seek antique jewelry calls for planning.

First, where are the shows and shops? Magazine and trade publications devoted to antiques, art, jewelry, and other collectibles are available on most newsstands (and always by subscription). In them you will find names and addresses of dealers in various towns and states, along with show listings and their dates and times.

Consulting local-event guides, local newspapers and local Yellow Pages of any town you are visiting is always a good way to net a list of local antique dealers. If you are browsing in an antiques arcade or building where a number of dealers are located, check each business and ask to be put on mailing lists to receive any flyers or brochures about future sales events. Ask for business cards from the dealers you visit and keep a card file. If you are looking for something special and the dealer does not have it, ask for a recommendation to another one who might. Of course, be warned that once you admit to searching for a particular object, the price may go up, sometimes beyond its true value.

Buying antique jewelry by mail is not a good idea. You will find in various jewelry, antique or society magazines ads of dealers who sell by mail and offer a money-back guarantee. And there are some antique-jewelry dealers who expand their shop business by mailing out offerings they think their customers might be interested in. Mail order is difficult for dealers who do only road shows, and this type of transaction is best avoided unless the dealers have a permanent address.

You might need to get a guarantee exercised.

If you must buy from an advertisement or mail solicitation, talk to the dealer on the telephone *before you send your check* and try to get clear information about the piece. Here are some important questions to ask:

▧ Is it genuine?

▧ Is it a good example of its period?

▧ Is it handmade or machine made?

▧ Is the workmanship good?

▧ What is the condition?

▧ Does it have gemstones? Have they been identified? Are they set securely?

▧ Will the dealer buy back any item identified mistakenly as to age or quality?

▧ Can you get a FAX photo of the piece (or photograph through the mail) front and back for a better judgment of its desirability?

## WHAT TO KNOW BEFORE BUYING ANTIQUE JEWELRY OVERSEAS

For those individuals lucky enough to be able to travel whenever and wherever they wish, antique-jewelry collecting in foreign countries offers exciting possibilities.

**London**—Both novice and experienced collectors often comment about the good buys they make in London, the best city in the world for antique-jewelry shopping. First of all, without the language barrier, shopping is made easier; and second, London has a seemingly limitless selection of antique jewelry, with greater variety of periods and styles than anywhere else in the world.

A woman gemologist living in Paris while on assignment with the U.S. State Department has spent much of her free time traveling to London to make a concerted search of the area's antique-jewelry markets. While discovering London's hidden treasures she has also organized a list of "must-see" antique shops and markets.

Here are her suggestions: Mayfair section antique shops; New Bond Street auction houses; Portobello Road antiques market on Saturday morning; Knightsbridge antique shops and museums; Chelsea antiques shops; and Marylebone, Islington, Bloomsbury, New Caledonia/Bermondsey (Friday only) markets.

The Bermondsey/New Caledonia Market is something really special. The markets open very early on Friday morning and is a combination outdoor/indoor market. Many antique dealers arrive to sell and trade among themselves before dawn and are gone from the area by 9:00 A.M. in order to open their own shops. Since it is generally still dark when the market opens, you should bring a flashlight with you. This tool will also identify you as a serious, knowledgeable antique buyer. Those who go regularly to this market promise that, if you know what you are looking for, you will find plenty of good deals.

Some affordable pieces collected in the London markets a few months ago include an Etruscan Revival locket brooch for $550 (see Fig. 4–22, Chapter 4), a pinchbeck brooch with red-glass stone for $50 (Fig. 6–1), a cut-steel brooch in a butterfly design for $100 (Fig. 1–3, Chapter 1), and a sapphire and diamond brooch of superb quality for $2,500 (Fig. 6–2). Although none of the items were hallmarked for exact circa dating, they all have easily identifiable features.

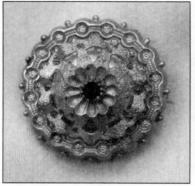

**Fig. 6–1** *(left) A pinchbeck brooch purchased in London at an affordable price; $50. (Photo by Peggy Blackford.)*

**Fig. 6–2** *(right) This London find at $2,500 is an Edwardian brooch in platinum on gold with diamonds and sapphires. (Photo by Peggy Blackford.)*

**Amsterdam**—We believe that shopping for antique jewelry in Holland is a well-kept secret of the Dutch! There is plenty around, and prices are significantly low, but finding a dealer is not easy. Of course, most shops located on those quaint and narrow streets in Holland will put a piece or two of antique jewelry in the window, but there are few dealers who sells *only* antique jewelry.

The reason was explained by a dealer in the village of Wassenaar: Antiquarian/jeweler Carien Wierda has her fine collection in her home and shows it by special invitation once a month. "The Dutch are very conservative," she said. "They usually own family pieces and do not buy many antique jewelry items. They prefer new, contemporary designer jewelry."

The jewelry in the shop of this Dutch dealer is mostly Victorian and Art Deco. Some truly outstanding buys can be made in mourning jewelry because, Wierda says, "The Dutch do not like the idea of having someone else's hair in their jewelry." An examination of a large display of hair jewelry revealed brooches, pendants, rings, and earrings dating about

Fig. 6–3 *(top right) The workmanship in antique Dutch jewelry is some of the finest to be found anywhere. These Victorian-era gold bracelets are not only solidly made, but are also beautifully decorated. (Courtesy Carien Wierda.)*

Fig. 6–4 *(top left) This mid-1800s gold brooch with blue enamel and half-pearls is in pristine condition. (Courtesy Carien Wierda.)*

Fig. 6–5 *(bottom right) Two examples from a case full of well-crafted gold antique pins found in Holland and affordably priced $200–$500. (Courtesy Carien Wierda.)*

1880 and ranging in price from $100 to $1,000. Several of the brooches had natural-pearl-edged mountings.

Other notable, affordable jewelry included a pair of gold bracelets (Fig. 6–3) in 15 karat gold for $500, a Victorian gold brooch with blue enamel and half-pearls for $1,000 (Fig. 6–4), and gold pins, finely decorated and excellently crafted ranging from $200 to $500 (Fig. 6–5). Of course there were some outstanding items that were well beyond our affordable range, like a 1700s Dutch-made diamond and silver pendant (Fig. 6–6, and 6–7). This piece, set with over 200 old-mine-cut diamonds with a total weight of 6 carats, exhibits fine workmanship and is in excellent condition. Asking price? Close to $7,000 U.S. dollars.

One warning from the Dutch dealer was about Dutch-

**Fig. 6–6** *(left) A magnificently crafted 1700s diamond and silver pendant by Dutch master jewelers. The piece is set with over 200 old-mine-cut diamonds. (Courtesy Carien Wierda.)*

**Fig. 6–7** *(right) The back view of the Dutch-made 1700s pendant shows a well-finished item. Note that the backs of the diamonds are closed, thus giving a circa-dating clue. (Courtesy Carien Wierda.)*

made antique-jewelry reproductions. They are almost impossible to separate from the original jewels because several firms are using their own original one-hundred-year-old molds, along with old gold-finishing techniques. They are even using rose-cut diamonds in the reproductions to fool the unwary.

**Paris**—Antique-jewelry hunting in Paris can be an unqualified success for those with plenty of time and francs. One of the better-known markets for high-quality antique jewelry is a shopping mall called Le Louvre de Antiquaires. Here, jewelry from Renaissance Revival, Edwardian, and Art Nouveau to Art Deco is abundant. Much of it is signed; most is hallmarked (Figs. 6–8, 6–9). Recent finds at this market include a hand-carved sardonyx cameo brooch in an elaborate 18K gold frame with table-cut diamonds; a diamond and cameo 18K yellow-gold stickpin; and jewelry in marcasite, tortoiseshell,

**Fig. 6–8** *(left) Shopping for antique jewelry overseas can produce some remarkable items, like this gold bird pin set with 264 rose-cut diamonds and 17 rubies. This pin was part of the Shah of Iran's collection. (Photo from the collection of The "Original" Classic International Gem & Jewelry Show, Inc.)*

**Fig. 6–9** *(right) Shopping in France, it is still possible to find historical jewelry items with documented provenance, like this gold and blue enamel ring given by Napoleon I to his mother (Madame Mère) upon the occasion of his coronation. The inscription on the enamel reads "Vive l'Empereur." The ring has Paris gold quality marks that date it circa 1803–1818. It was given to Madame Mère in 1804. (Photo from the collection of The "Original" Classic International Gem & Jewelry Show, Inc.)*

and jet. Only the marcasite jewelry, priced at a few hundred dollars, fell into our affordable category.

The famous Parisian flea market, Marché aux Puces, however, provides plenty of shops selling affordable antique jewelry alongside contemporary pieces, and an enormous quantity of costume jewelry.

Some recent finds there include a demantoid garnet and diamond ring in 18K yellow gold for $900, and a pair of 18K circa 1824 gold earrings priced at $1,400. The earrings were sensational finds if they were actually what the seller claimed as Charles X vintage. They looked *brand new* which—according to the seller—was due to the fact that they (along with an 18K gold and enamel ring from the eighteenth century, price $1,000) had just been discovered languishing in a jeweler's safe!

Rewards of a careful hunt turned up an 18K yellow-gold-and-enamel bird brooch for $500; and a silver-on-18K-gold brooch engraved with an Aesop fable for $1,000.

# ABOUT THE *VAT* TAX

In most Western European countries, the Value Added Tax will be included on quoted prices. You may be able to get a refund of this tax which may range from 18 to 20 percent or more, depending upon the country you are visiting.

In Great Britain, where you are most likely to be doing antique-jewelry shopping, you should get a VAT Tax form from the dealer from whom you are buying. This form will be stamped by British customs upon your leaving the country, and it is up to you to put it in a mailbox for delivery back to the dealer *before you leave the country*. If you ask, the dealer you are buying from will probably give you a stamped envelope along with your VAT Tax form, so that after Customs stamps it, you have only to drop it into the airport mailbox. If you do not want to get a refund in British pounds—and possibly lose money in exchanging it for U.S. currency—pay for your purchases by credit card. Then when the dealer receives the documents you mailed, he or she can issue credit on your card. This technique not only saves you money, but unnecessary paperwork and headaches over refunds.

If the jewelry you have bought overseas is antique—that is, over 100 years old—and its age is duly noted by the seller on your receipt, you do not have to pay duty upon entry into the United States. However, although antiques are admitted duty free, you still must declare your purchases and be prepared to prove their age with the proper documentation.

Jewelry buyers should skip jewelry and artifacts made from skins, shells, feathers, or teeth of endangered species. While some beautiful and interesting jewelry may be found in markets all over the world, these materials may be classified as coming from endangered species and thus are illegal to bring into the United States. Trying to bring them home puts you at risk of their seizure by U.S. government inspectors and a possible fine. Check with U.S. Customs before you go abroad and get its pamphlet about products you cannot bring into the country. Otherwise you risk losing some precious bargains.

There are also strict laws, especially in Mediterranean and Eastern European countries against export of their national treasures, which include jewelry. Although many pieces are sold within their own countries quite legally, it is strictly forbidden to take such treasures out of the country.

# $\mathcal{D}$RESSING
## FOR THE
# $\mathcal{H}$UNT

## IN THE EYE OF THE BEHOLDER

Did you notice how people dress to go shopping? To attend sports events? To the theater? Well, antique hunting is like theater, and there is an appropriate costume to be worn by players in the buying game. You may have never read about such rules in a book on buying antiques of any kind. You may not have given it any thought yourself, but ponder for a moment: How do you look as a buyer to a seller? Consider the psychology of dressing and how what you wear affects how the seller sees you.

A parallel might be drawn to expert witnesses and jurors. Expert witnesses for jewelry and gemstone cases are told to dress conservatively. Specifically, they are advised to wear dark suits, white shirts, and plain ties for men—no sport jackets. For women, the code is a tailored, simple dress. Both sexes are cautioned not to wear eye-catching jewelry, with a special advice against expensive wristwatches. The rationale behind this requirement for austerity is that a juror who has to take time off from his job and lose much-needed pay, may easily become resentful and prejudiced against an expert witness's luxurious jewelry. This is what is called dress psychology.

Even though it is irrational, people *are judged* by the way they dress. When you are shopping in a fine department store or an upscale antique establishment and want immediate help from salesclerks, *dress up!* Wear a dress or suit, hose and heels, and accessorize your outfit with your own antique jewelry or estate pieces. It is miraculous how much attention and respect you get from the staff and management when you are dressed fashionably. If, however, you enter a jewelry store, department store, or a fine antique store wearing a running suit, jeans, or shorts and tennis shoes, you are virtually ignored (especially if your attire is not squeaky fresh). The staff's perception is that you are not serious about buying. When you are waited on, the staff politeness is rather perfunctory and rude, since you are considered to be nobody with no money to spend. (Although this perception has been proven false in many cases, it is a reality just the same.)

But when you are going antique shopping at flea markets, garage sales, house-tag sales, mall antique sales, or just country browsing, *dressing down* is the answer. You are after bargains, aren't you? If you arrive with all your jewelry flashing and jangling and dressed as if for high tea, you will be spotted as a tourist and "easy touch." Best dress for antique shows is middle ground. For women, blouses and skirts and tennis shoes are permitted. After all, the world has labeled most women antique hunters as little old ladies in tennis shoes, and we wouldn't want to disappoint them!

# TOO MANY COOKS
# SPOIL THE BROTH

Of course, not all antique hunters are little old ladies. Some are young ladies and men, and sometimes they attend antique shows, flea markets, and garage sales... with the family tagging along.

This is no way to shop. While it is fine for children to get an early introduction to and education about antiques, looking for antique jewelry is a serious business for collectors and should not be hampered by too many outside influences. Similarly, two women shopping together is poor logistics if the purpose of the hunt is to augment a collection. When two women shop together, they tend to cancel each other out either in a well-meaning way or by design. Retailers will tell you that they are loath to see two women come into the shop together because when one says to the other, "How do you like this?" the answer—inevitably—is no, and the sale will be killed. When a woman shops for antique jewelry with her husband, if he is not equally involved in the hunt, he is usually in a hurry or bored. Either way, his attitude keeps his wife from fully investigating and examining the piece for sale.

Children require almost constant supervision and steer the grown-ups' attention away from antiques to themselves. Otherwise, tots' "activities" in an antique store can turn what was supposed to be a pleasure into a disastrous—and costly—experience.

In the end, a woman collector shopping alone and dressed for the part stands the best chance of finding, examining, bargaining, and purchasing the best in antique jewelry.

# LESSONS IN BARGAINING—
## IT NEVER HURTS TO ASK

Bargaining is a way of life almost all over the world except in the United States and a few Western European countries. It is a perfectly respectable practice that makes common sense and is not an indication that you are poor. As a matter of fact, most dealers know well that some of the best deals are struck by their wealthiest clients.

Americans are easily embarrassed about trying to reduce marked prices even in countries where bargaining is expected. In Southern Europe, Asia, the Near East, Mexico, and South America, haggling is a natural way of life. It is expected, and if it does not happen the seller feels deprived of part of the enjoyment of his day.

In upscale establishments, housed in high-rent districts, first-class shopping malls and office buildings, you must expect comparatively high prices in order for the store owners to cover their overhead. Bargaining is usually not welcome here, and often an arrogant sales staff will tell you so sharply.

Let me remind you that antique hunting is supposed to be *fun*, not a pressure-filled or an intimidating undertaking. As a new gemologist attending gem shows, I remember that dealers were ruthlessly intimidating. They were emphatic in their pronouncements that the gems they were trying to sell were "the best," "the only," and sometimes, "the last ones left" in the entire world! The strategy used by the seller was aimed to stampede or panic a buyer into a purchase. The identical scenario applies to antique jewelry. While truly ancient jewelry is in finite supply, most mass-produced pieces that make up our affordable collectibles are plentiful. So do not be afraid to bargain because you might miss a good buy;

remember, on the other side of the showcase is a dealer who is just as disturbed by the prospect of missing a sale! Many antique-jewelry dealers advertise they sell to the public at wholesale or trade prices. You can ask, but you will probably not win more than a 10 percent collector discount from them.

Beware of some bargain dealers. Sometimes their bargains are not good values for the money, and a lot of the stock may be fakes and/or reproduction pieces. If a dealer offers you a big discount on an item after little or no bargaining, inspect it carefully. The discount may be the dealer's way to temp you to buy quickly without taking time to authenticate the piece as genuine. One high-pressure tactic is to put time constraints on an item ("only good at this price till noon") or to hint that it is the only one of its kind.

Here are a few bargaining tips:

※ Understand that the dealer's quoted price is the maximum figure he hopes to realize. What this means to you is that some dealers put a figure (price) on a piece of antique jewelry as their guide and what they think the market will bear. Sometimes the amount asked is pure guesswork. Often the guide is what comparable items have recently sold for in the market.

If the dealer has had the piece for a long time (over six months), or if it is the end of the month and rent is coming due and other overhead expenses must be met, the dealer will usually be happy to reduce the price.

※ Do not go into a bargaining session with your body language sending signals that you will pay the asking price but are "hoping" to get a discount. You must be self-assured and slightly aggressive, but don't overdo it!

※ *Never* tell what price you are prepared to pay! An astute dealer will probe to find out your limit, but keep it to yourself. Do, however, have a sum in mind that is an acceptable top price, but try to find out what the dealer's lowest price is. If you are negotiating, increase your offer in small increments.

## ASKING THE RIGHT QUESTIONS—GETTING THE RIGHT ANSWERS

What is the *right* discount?

There is no "right" discount because of the great variation in circumstances surrounding the selling and buying of antique jewelry, but most buyers who are bargaining offer about a third less than the asking price. For example, if a piece of jewelry is marked at $1,500 and the maximum you are prepared to pay is $1,250, offer the dealer $1,000, with the expectation that you might be able to settle around $1,200.

Never put yourself in a position where you are pressured to accept a price above *your* maximum price.

When should you walk away?

You should be able to walk away from any deal where, after you have disclosed your maximum price, the dealer still refuses your offer. After all, you must consider just how much the item is worth to you. Bargaining is a game full of bluff and showmanship tactics. Most of all, do not lose the psychological advantage you have as buyer by communicating to the seller how desperate you are for the item. You may need to resort to the tactics used by the best hagglers in the world in both the Egyptian and Turkish bazaars and Mexican markets...walk away. If they really want to sell, they will quickly capitulate or counter with a better offer than before.

A bargaining ploy used in Turkish bazaars is pulling out your money at the critical point where you feel the seller is near a deal. Timing is crucial, and you should not reach for your money too soon. However, sometimes the visibility of cash clinches the bargain. In the most famous bazaar in the world, the Istanbul Grand Bazaar, you will find world-class hagglers. In fact, even when the price of an item has been fully agreed upon and you stand with cash in hand waiting while the merchant wraps the item, the negotiating continues!

It is all part of the daily selling routine and is expected. And, psychologically, isn't it a lot more fun to have bought an item at a discount price? Even if it is only a small, token cash amount, a discount makes you feel like a world-class bargain hunter!

## CHAPTER EIGHT

# Collecting

## BY THE

# Book

## HOW TO START A COLLECTION

Some shoppers admit that they got interested in searching for antique jewelry because of a gift or purchase of a single piece, but most simply have no idea how to get started in antique jewelry. Often novice collectors take the "Christopher Columbus approach" by just heading out in a straight line for an unknown destination (goal), weaving in and out of various markets and finally hitting—or finding—something that pleases them.

A good example and outcome of the Columbus approach is the story of a female collector who, after buying an antique garnet brooch, decided that she wanted a close match in a ring. She and her husband joined the crowds making the rounds of antique shops, shows, and flea markets. Two weeks after her shopping frenzy, the woman had over twenty garnet pieces lined up on her dresser. She picked out the ones she was fondest of with the best color match and began wearing them daily as her "signature" jewelry; the rest—never worn—languish in a box at home. She laughs at some of the pieces she bought years ago, haphazardly and out of emotion: "My eye and taste have really changed," she says. "I would not buy the same things today that I did then. I have become more educated about antique jewelry and a more experienced buyer."

Her story is not new. Many first-time buyers start with the single desire to adorn their bodies. They learn a lot along the way, and their tastes change. The problem seems to be how to start productively but keep down what can become a very expensive education. Once the jewelry is purchased, unless you are a dealer, it may be very difficult to recycle it— to sell it back.

Many buy purely from emotion: "I like it, I want it." A Florida collector cautions that antique-jewelry buying is a lot like buying art. "It is something that you enjoy more over a longer period of time spent collecting it; you can even become quite passionate about collecting."

One Texas dealer says, "A lot of people are intimidated when they come looking at antique jewelry. They cannot make up their minds and use the excuse that they do not know anything about antique jewelry." She recalls a woman who admitted that, while she knew next to nothing about buying antique jewelry, she was inexplicably drawn to Victorian bow brooches. The dealer said, "I told her that is fine, and that is all there is to buying. You need to get some emotional feeling from what you are looking at—just like looking at art." The same dealer tells her customers that if they are uncertain about buying an item, they probably have not seen enough antique jewelry and should look around some more.

Emotion is fine to sustain growth of a collection, but what is really needed to start and build a collection is a sound buying plan.

## BUILDING WITH A PLAN

The number-one rule of building a notable—and wearable—collection is always to buy at the top of your budget. Junk jewelry will always be junk, whether it is antique or contemporary.

One of the oldest museum adages is to collect to strength. That means that several pieces of jewelry from the same period or designer, or of the same type, make a more memorable group than many scattered single items ranging over the centuries.

Decide which period of the past is of special interest to you. If money is a factor, consider the gemstones that are not currently in vogue and thus are more affordable.

## COLLECTING A SINGLE ITEM OR PERIOD

A woman buying in the antique market in London not long ago noticed a shiny metal gemlike brooch and purchased it along with a book on Victorian jewelry. When she got home, she read about her acquisition and found out she had old marcasite jewelry. Before her purchase, marcasite and old Berlin iron jewelry had seemed completely uninteresting to her. However, because she found beauty and historic value in her marcasite brooch, she succeeded within a relatively short time in assembling a collection of marcasite jewelry unparalleled for its representation of well-preserved examples. This collector lectures on her specialty and declares that not only is collecting antique jewelry a joy to the senses, but also a way to expand the collector's knowledge of history and make his or her jewelry serve as a time machine that brings the past alive in the present.

Of course you can be too famous a collector at times—or at least too well known. Dr. Joe Sataloff, a Philadelphia physician/collector and connoisseur of Art Nouveau jewelry, delights in telling a story about himself and his collecting adventures:

One day when he and his wife Ruth were walking around the jewelry district in New York City searching for Art Nouveau jewelry, he spotted a beautiful example of a brooch of that period in a store window. From what he could tell, the piece was in pristine condition, with beautiful jewellike enamel and design in the wispy curvilear style characteristic of Art Nouveau. It looked like a fine addition to his collection, so Sataloff and his wife walked into the store and inquired about the price of the piece. The proprietor looked up from his work and said that the item was not for sale. Puzzled at the brooch's being shown openly in the window, Dr. Sataloff asked why it was not for sale.

"Oh," the dealer explained with a shrug, "we are keeping it around in case a rich and crazy doctor/collector from Philadelphia comes in. We heard he will buy at any price!"

## WHEN AND HOW TO GET INSURANCE

To protect yourself from loss of your antique jewelry in a fire, burglary, or accident, you should purchase insurance coverage. The agent who handles your homeowners' or tenants' insurance can also write an endorsement—sometimes called rider, schedule, or floater—to your existing policy, which will specify the value of each piece of jewelry covered.

If you have the choice, an *Agreed Value* policy is what you should buy. Discuss this option with your agent. State insurance codes vary, and companies are limited in what they write. An Agreed Value policy guarantees that, if you have a claim, you will receive the full amount (full price) stated on the appraisal document. You must obtain an appraisal before such a rider can be included in your policy.

A good appraisal will ensure that the jewelry is covered for *full replacement value*—in other words, how much it would cost in the current retail antique-jewelry market to either replace the individual item with an identical one (if it is available), or with a comparable item. Understand what kind of coverage you are buying before you purchase; talk with your insurance agent at length and have him or her answer all your questions.

## HOW TO GET AN APPRAISAL

Because society—and therefore collecting its treasures—has gotten more complex over the past few decades, the appraising profession has advanced at a rapid rate. People acquiring personal property such as jewelry, albeit one piece or an entire collection, want to protect it.

Fortunately, the public is demanding more information and asking more questions these days of the people who serve it. The public understands little of the art and science that goes into jewelry appraising or in estimating the value of an item. For an appraisal for insurance coverage, replacement of the jewelry depends largely on the complete and accurate description. An appraisal that reads "One, circa 1840 yellow gold English bracelet" is not good enough for the accurate replacement of lost or stolen goods. The description on your appraisal document should include the metal identification and weight, design of the mounting, cut and quality and estimated weight of any gemstones, condition of the piece, circa date, hallmarks, manufacturer's mark, description of quality of workmanship and manufacturing method. To ensure as accurate a replacement as possible, there should also be a photograph of the item attached to the appraisal report.

Not all jewelry appraisers have the knowledge and expertise to value antique jewelry. Ask questions of the appraiser such as:

🔅 What is your appraisal educational background?

🔅 What specific experience do you have with antique-jewelry appraising?

🔅 Are you a member of an appraisal society such as the American Society of Appraisers?

🔅 How do you charge? (Responsible appraisal societies consider it unethical and unprofessional to charge a percentage of the appraised value.)

Do not hesitate to ask questions prior to selecting your appraiser; the professional practitioner will be pleased to answer and to place his or her qualifications before you. If you want more information or help in finding an appraiser, call or write the American Society of Appraisers, P.O. Box 17265, Washington, D.C. 20041.

## MAKING A PERSONAL INVENTORY

Keeping a good record of all the items in your collection is an organized way to keep track of what you own, what you paid for it, and where you bought it. Having a file consisting of an index card for each object will also help you determine whether the piece has appreciated since it was purchased.

The index card with receipt of purchase stapled to it should include information such as the dealer you bought it from and when, the circa date of the item, manufacturer—if known—hallmarks and provenance if it is known. If the item was purchased at auction, write down the date and lot number, and any description the auction house may have used in the catalog.

While this may seem like a lot of needless bother to casual collectors, a personal inventory will be permanent and valuable information which can make the difference between getting full value or not when your collection is up for sale either by you or your heirs.

## USING JEWELRY PRICE GUIDES

It does not take long for the buyer of antique jewelry to find out about price guides. There is a plethora of such publications on the market for items ranging from costume jewelry to royal jewels. Almost every general antiques price guide has a section on jewelry, and auction-house yearbooks cover sales with prices realized for entire years, even decades.

There is a danger in price guides, however, and that is

the tendency by buyers to accept the prices quoted as gospels, instead of just as guides to general pricing of similar or identical items. One guide—*The Antiques World*—warns readers that prices of individual antique-jewelry pieces can vary up to 50 percent or more, depending on the location of the market, the condition of the piece, and the eagerness of the purchaser. Do not ignore this caveat.

The location of the individual buyer is especially important. What is considered a hot buy in one state may not be even remotely interesting to buyers across the state line. Any jewelry that is provincial—that is, made by artists or craftsmen in a local area—will invariably bring higher prices in its own hometown or village. People are sensitive to history and tend to be sentimental about local productions, which creates a strong market for such pieces. Any item from the workshop of Paul Revere will bring a much higher price in Boston and the Northeast than in the South or West. The notable exceptions are the internationally acclaimed designers and manufacturers of antique jewelry.

Always consider the condition of a piece when looking over auction prices; emotions generated in an auction can distort the market value of a piece. Two bidders locked in a heated battle for an item of antique jewelry can shoot up the selling price well beyond its true market value. Therefore, auction prices are to be used only as guides.

Read over the front pages of any price guides before you turn to the inside material. Many authors will tell you exactly how the book is to be used and how their prices were derived.

## CHAPTER NINE

# LOST TREASURES
# YOU CAN FIND!

There is hardly any venture more exciting than setting out in search of antique jewelry that is rare or unusual. Every expedition of this kind is an adventure, and every shop or auction holds promise of the possibility of a real find, a bargain, a treasure rescued from the past.

Even if you do not find much on an individual journey into the antiques market, one of the most fascinating aspects of the search is the things you *will* see and what you learn.

We already know that most jewelry treasures have a story to tell, and sometimes the story is more fascinating than the piece itself. Collectors should be just as eager to seek the story behind the jewel, especially if it is historic, signed, or made by a noted artist.

There are many legends and stories about missing jewelry and gemstones—a few more fiction than fact—that are intriguing enough to recount here in hopes of enlivening the hunt for antique-jewelry treasures.

# THE BRUNSWICK DIAMOND
# FEATHER PIN

The central gemstone in this missing pin is a brilliant-cut lemon-yellow diamond, of Indian origin. The diamond has a documented and famous past as part of the treasure collection of the Duke of Brunswick, Charles II (1804–1873). He was unpopular in his duchy and was ousted by a younger brother. Moving to Geneva, Charles set about collecting an extraordinary cabinet of diamonds of which the brilliant yellow diamond was his favorite. He is reported to have once refused $60,000 for it; after his death, at the auction of his property, Tiffany & Company's Gideon F. T. Reed of the Paris branch purchased the Brunswick yellow diamond for the small sum of $8,000.

The designers at Tiffany had already decided the gemstone would be perfect set as the eye of a peacock-feather pin that could also serve as an aigrette for the hair.

The pin/aigrette was designed with diamonds encircling the eye in the feather in yellow gold, surrounded by another circle of diamonds in red gold. Along with the yellow diamond, the pin was also set with 600 fine white diamonds.

The Brunswick pin is in a platinum and multicolor gold frame. All the diamond settings are open in back to allow the greatest gemstone refraction and scintillation. Tiffany showed the pin at the Philadelphia Centennial Exhibition in 1876; at that time, it was valued at $15,000; the other jewelry exhibited by Tiffany along with the Brunswick pin was valued at $300,000. However, it was the Brunswick pin/aigrette that received the most accolades from the press and public, and Tiffany won several awards for its design. An engraving (Fig. 9–1) was made for use in the exhibition catalog and in jewelry magazines, but unfortunately no other drawings or engrav-

**Fig. 9–1** *An engraving of the Brunswick pin is the only pictorial record of this treasure. (Courtesy Dover Publishing.)*

ings were made or can be found of the piece.

After the centennial closed, Tiffany displayed the Brunswick pin/aigrette in its store in Union Square. It was not long before other jewelers copied the design, but later versions of the piece featured fewer diamonds, and various stones—especially the moonstone—were used as substitutes for the yellow diamond.

The whereabouts of this piece are not known today. While it may have been sold or broken up and its diamonds reused in other jewelry, Tiffany has no record of its sale or breakup.

The Brunswick pin is a Victorian-era treasure to search for. It may be lying unrecognized in some dealer's showcase, or may be a forgotten and unappreciated object in a flea market or estate sale.

## THE BRUNSWICK BLUE DIAMOND

Charles II also owned a 13.75 carat blue pear-shape diamond that was put up for sale in 1874 in Geneva. It was purchased by the Parisian company of Ochs Brothers, which paid $163,200 for it. At the time, some experts believed that the Brunswick Blue and the Hope diamonds had both come from the recutting of the Blue Diamond of the Crown because the two blue gemstones were identical in quality and color. However, other experts maintained that it was a technical impossibility to cut a 13.75-carat pear-shape diamond and a 44.50-carat cushion-shape diamond from what was known to be a 67.13-carat heart-shape stone. The whereabouts of the Brunswick Blue diamond is completely unknown. It may be set and unrecognized in the head of a walking stick or in the center of a pendant or ring, and owned by someone for whom it is *just a blue stone*. Or it may be lying about in a box of unset and unidentified jewels. You could be the lucky finder!

## THE FLORENTINE DIAMOND

There are hundreds of reports of famous missing diamonds, but few are more romantic than that of the great yellow diamond known as the Florentine, the only diamond in the world with an Italian name. The 137.27 carat gemstone is fashioned in the form of an irregular nine-sided, 126-facet double-rose-cut (Fig. 9–2). Its provenance goes back to 1477, when Charles the Bold, Duke of Burgundy was wearing it when he was felled in the Battle of Nancy. The diamond was removed from the duke's body by a soldier or peasant who, believing it to be glass, sold it to a priest for a florin. The diamond changed owners many times; one of the owners was Pope Julius II (1503–1513).

Reports about the Florentine diamond date from 1657, when Jean-Baptiste Tavernier, the famous French gem dealer, saw the stone while he was visiting the Medici family in Florence. From there the diamond passed to Vienna to the

Grand Duke of Tuscany and his wife Empress Maria Theresa, and then to the House of Hapsburg, where it was set in the Hapsburg crown.

After World War I and the fall of the Austro-Hungarian Empire, the Florentine diamond was mounted in a brooch and went with the rest of the crown jewels into exile in Switzerland with the imperial family.

**Fig. 9–2** *The Florentine diamond is a nine-sided 126-facet double-rose-cut stone.*

The rest of the story of the Florentine is clouded in romantic fact—or perhaps romantic fiction. It was reportedly stolen by an adviser to the imperial family and taken to South America, from where the brooch was supposed to have been sent into the United States in about 1920. Complete mystery surrounds the stone from that time on, and whether it was recut and sold is not known. Both stone and brooch are officially listed as missing.

# EMERALD NECKLACE-PENDANT FROM THE HOUSE OF SAVOY

An emerald necklace-pendant, part of the House of Savoy crown jewels, and likely to be part of the missing Italian Dongo Treasure may be resting unknown somewhere in the United States.

This piece, made in Palermo, Italy over 200 years ago, features 68 diamonds, a 23.5-carat emerald set in the center, and nine other emeralds, along with natural pearls (Fig. 9–3) in the chain. The mounting is silver layered over 18 karat yel-

**Fig. 9–3** *The last-known photograph of the missing emerald pendant that was part of the House of Savoy crown jewels. (Courtesy Ben Noble, Jr.— Gemological consultant.)*

low gold, typical of its period of crafting.

Valued at more than $200,000 in 1950, the piece was a gift to Mussolini from Queen Elena of Italy in the early part of the twentieth century. It was meant to be a gift for Mussolini's wife, but Il Duce decided instead to give it as a love token to his mistress Clara Petacci.

Not only is it part of the House of Savoy jewels but it is also rumored to have been part of the Dongo Treasure, a treasure cache hidden away by Mussolini at the end of World War II, the whereabouts of which are still shrouded in mystery. Most of the treasure has never been recovered.

In 1946, Il Duce—along with his money, art, precious possessions, mistress Clara and some prominent Fascists—fled toward Switzerland. Even though he was disguised, Mussolini did not escape, and both he and Clara were seized, executed, and hanged by their heels in a small town called Messegra. Although it is known that at the time of her death Petacci was wearing the emerald treasure, it is not known precisely who removed it from her body or who whisked it away and hid it. But in 1947 the piece turned up mysteriously in California as part of a cache of goods smuggled illegally into the United States.

The trail picks up again in 1954 in Texas, where the necklace-pendant, after being displayed in a bank lobby, was sold to a wealthy industrialist and his wife. The lady made a grand show of wearing it to the opening night of both the opera and symphony, and the piece has not been seen publicly since. After the couple divorced, a few years later, there was no more news about the piece. The woman traveled abroad extensively and eventually remarried. Her mysterious death in Florida a few months after her second marriage also caused speculation about the disappearance of the jewel.

Where is the necklace-pendant today? No one knows. Perhaps it waits for you to rescue it from obscurity in some antique shop where the dealer does not realize how historically important the piece is.

# THE ROSSETTI
# POCKET WATCH

The worldwide search for this pocket watch was kicked off in 1990 during conversation with Geoffrey C. Munn, the author of *Artists' Jewellery*. Munn explained that he and his coauthor had been searching for the watch but were stymied after tracing it from Great Britain to the United States. It is someplace in Florida, he believes.

Perhaps you will be the lucky collector to uncover the mystery of the whereabouts of this spectacular piece.

The watch was designed by English painter and poet Dante Gabriel Rossetti (1828–1882), one of the founders of the Pre-Raphaelite Brotherhood credited with important accomplishments in art and literature. Rossetti's paintings were romantic, and strong on beautiful draped models wearing magnificent jewelry, much of which he owned. Some of the Rossetti jewelry survives, bequeathed to the Victoria and Albert Museum, and many of the items have been matched with those seen in his paintings. Some, however, have been lost, including the Indian pearl earrings worn by models in several of his pictures. For a man intensely interested in jewelry, it seems odd that he himself drew only two jewelry designs, both for watch cases. Eventually the watches were made, and the whereabouts of one of the slim gold timepieces has piqued the interest of connoisseurs and collectors for several decades.

The missing watch is in a design commissioned by Edward Robert Robson and manufactured in 1863 by Cozens, Matthews & Thorpe; it bears the number 96674. The gold pocket watch is decorated with black champlevé enamel on the case and dial. The design on the front of the watch is decidedly medieval; the subject is "Time on the Wing."

Opposite a backdrop of stars, a sun and quarter-moon are centered on the watch face; within the sun is a three-quarter face of a crowned king with the legend SOL; the quarter-moon—with an evening star at the bottom tip—is filled out by the profile of a woman and the legend LUNA; both rest winged atop a sixty-second-hand dial. The numerals are arabic. The back of the case is Oriental in design; the motif is Japanese: a long-beaked bird with wings extended in flight against a background of flowers.

Mr. Robson willed the Rossetti-designed timepiece to his son Philip Appleby Robson. Although numerous inquiries have been made among the Robson family, the whereabouts of this gold watch is a mystery.

## THE QUEDLINBURG TREASURE

Religious treasures are ideal to look for during your search for antique jewelry. There are hundreds of missing ancient reliquaries (containers made in precious metals and ornamented with gemstones). These pieces were made with particularly loving care because they held relics of saints—most often a piece of bone, a strand of hair, or few drops of blood. Some are even said to contain a splinter of wood which is allegedly a piece of the "true cross." They are all considered sacred objects. Countless lost or stolen reliquaries could show up at anytime and anywhere, perhaps at the next auction you attend. They are frequently overlooked because few people know what they actually represent. Small and portable, many have been carried to the United States by priests who came to this country hundreds of years ago and later, bought surreptitiously by collectors. Some were taken as war booty.

In 1991 it was revealed that a group of priceless religious treasures taken from a German church at the end of World War II had surfaced in Whitewright, Texas. How did they get there? An American soldier, Lt. Joe T. Meador, found the objects in a mineshaft, where they had been stored near Quedlinburg during the war. These objects of gold, silver, ivory, and crystal had been recognized for more than 1,000 years as some of the most important pieces of eighth- to six-teenth-century religious art in Germany. The treasures included work from the rule of Charlemagne and Otto I. Among them was a nineth- to tenth-century carved ivory comb inlaid with precious gems from the period of Germany's second king, Henry I, the Saxon king who united the German states and whose son Otto I was the first Holy Roman Emperor. It was Henry who established the convent of St. Servatius, which later became the Lutheran Church of Quedlinburg, the owner of the treasure. Other pieces included a crystal reliquary inscribed in Latin as containing a hair of the Virgin Mary, donated by Emperor Otto III.

After Joe Meador returned to the United States with the artifacts, he worked in the family hardware store in Whitewright, Texas. While some people recall seeing the items displayed in the store, Meador never tried to sell any of the objects. After his death in 1980, his heirs attempted to sell the pieces and finally managed to dispose of a medieval bible, the *Samuhel Gospel*, to the German Cultural Foundation of the United States. After that sale, a German investigator traced the remainder of the lost art to the Meador heirs. In early 1992, the German church of Quedlinburg and the Meador family settled the matter, and the treasure returned to Germany after a substantial cash settlement was paid for their return.

But that is not the end of the matter. It now appears that two pieces are still missing from the Quedlinburg Treasure

**Fig. 9–4** *Can you find this missing treasure? If you do, the German church of Quedlinburg wants it back. (Photograph courtesy Pfarrer Friedemann GoBlau.)*

**Fig. 9–5** *This missing Byzantine cross is a twelfth- or thirteenth-century treasure; it may be someplace in the U.S. (Photograph courtesy Pfarrer Friedemann GoBlau.)*

and while they may be in Texas, their actual whereabouts are unknown. Maybe you can find them. The German Church wants them back and no doubt will be generous in its reward for return.

One piece is a small 9.2 x 7.7 cm rock-crystal reliquary (Fig. 9–4) carved in the shape of a miter (bishop's hat). The carved crystal portion dates from the fourth century, while the gold-gilt silver mountings have been recorded as fourteenth-century work. There is an undeciphered Latin inscription on the mounting. The piece is small enough for someone to mistake it for a large pendant, especially as it appears to have a bail fitted at the top of the crystal that can easily accommodate a chain.

The second missing item is a large Byzantine cross, hinged to open (Fig. 9–5). The twelfth- to thirteenth-century cross is wrought of a gold-gilt over copper material with blue cloisonné enamel ornamentation. Depicted on the front of the cross is a haloed Jesus Christ with outstretched arms; on the reverse is a blue and white cloisonné-enameled field of flowers. The cross is fitted with a large bail at the top so it can be hung on a chain.

There is no doubt that these missing pieces of the Quedlinburg Treasure belong to a very special group of medieval masterpieces that have survived for centuries. They will surface again, someplace in the United States. Look for them.

## CHAPTER TEN

# CARING FOR YOUR ANTIQUE JEWELRY

Do as little cleaning of your antique jewelry as possible. If you absolutely *must* clean a piece, take it to a responsible and trusted jeweler *who also sells* antique jewelry. But, before you leave your property, talk to the jeweler at length about what he/she proposes to do. Antique jewelry should *never* be steam-cleaned or put into an ultrasonic cleaning machine. A steam cleaner is too harsh and will remove the patina that is one of the distinguishing features of antique jewelry. An ultrasonic cleaner works on vibration and can damage your jewelry in a number of ways:

(1) Stones may fall out of their settings or crack.

(2) Oil may leach (leak) out of oiled gemstones.

(3) Color may be pulled out of dyed gemstones.

(4) Organic gemstones such as coral, tortoiseshell, pearls,

amber, jet; and soft stones like turquoise and lapis lazuli will be destroyed.

(5) Foil-backed stones will be destroyed.

(6) Hair jewelry will be destroyed.

If you want to clean away a little dust, do it with a soft baby toothbrush and a soft, dry cloth. Many lockets have pictures inside that may be damaged by wet or damp cleaning. Enameled jewelry also requires careful handling. Soft enamels may easily be washed out of settings when they are treated harshly. Dampness must be avoided because moisture can activate acid and salts and, if the base metal is copper, water will corrode it and the enamel will be displaced. Hard enamels may be able to withstand gentle hand cleaning, but the emphasis is on the word *gentle*.

Here are some pointers for caring for the organic gemstones often found in antique jewelry:

*Amber* is a million-year-old fossilized resin and is very soft. It is easily attacked by acids. To clean amber, rinse it in lukewarm water and dry it carefully with a soft cloth. Heat is the enemy of amber, so store it away from direct sunlight or heat of any kind.

*Coral* is also a soft material which scratches very easily and can be ruined by numerous cleaning agents. For that reason, take no chances with coral and rinse only in lukewarm water and dry with a soft cloth.

*Ivory* is organic and will naturally turn yellowish with age. (Caveat: being yellow does *not* prove age or that the material is genuine ivory.) The color change is irreversible and desirable in antique jewelry. Exposure to heat, as well as prolonged exposure to dampness, will damage ivory. Clean ivory by rinsing it quickly in lukewarm water, followed by immediate thorough drying with a soft, dry cloth.

*Lava* is found in numerous pieces of antique jewelry in

the form of cameos. It is not only elegant and desirable but, unfortunately, impossible to clean. The lava may be in one of several colors from yellowish to black. Lava is very porous material, and *no cleaning agent or water* should be used. Brush it gently with a soft toothbrush or makeup brush to remove excess dust.

*Pearls* are damaged easily by heat, perfume, hair spray, and body oils. Pearls should be handled very gently and cleaned only by wiping them with a damp cloth and then drying them thoroughly with a soft, dry cloth. Most antique-pearl strands are extremely fragile and can be broken easily. Look closely at the silk or cotton string on your strand of pearls and, if it looks even slightly frayed, take it to a professional for restringing.

*Shell* is most often seen in mother-of-pearl articles that you should handle with the same care that you give to your pearls. Shell cameos should be cleaned only with a soft *dry* brush followed by gentle wiping with a soft, dry cloth. The modeled and carved features on shell cameos can be damaged beyond repair by harsh and aggressive cleaning methods.

*Tortoiseshell* is found in many pieces of Victorian and other old and antique-jewelry items. It is especially attractive when used in the piqué (inlay) jewelry articles. Treat this material gently and avoid extremes of temperature. Clean tortoiseshell *only* by gentle rubbing with a damp cloth.

# TAKING CARE OF
# COSTUME JEWELRY

It is smart today to collect old costume jewelry, even though it cannot be termed "antique." It is, however, highly collectible and is available and affordable from estate sales, flea markets and specialty dealers. This type of jewelry has its own special care, and collectors use these cleaning products: soft-bristle toothbrush, silver cloth that specifies "safe for gold," chamois cloth, glass cleaner, silver polish, and baking soda. This is the recommended cleaning procedure:

Brush jewelry gently with toothbrush to loosen dirt, especially around prongs and settings. Do this over a paper towel so if the stones are loose and fall out, they will not be lost. Use silver polish and a clean cloth for sterling and silver-plated jewelry. Buff with a chamois. If you are cleaning vermeil (gold layered over silver or other base metal) use only a cloth that says it is safe for gold so that you do not damage the gold gilt finish—it will rub off.

Clean crystal jewelry (glass) which has open-back settings with a glass cleaner like Windex. Rub dry with a soft cloth and buff with a chamois cloth. You cannot use glass cleaner or any liquid when cleaning foil-backed stones, however, because if liquid seeps into the backing, the backs will mildew, blacken, and disintegrate.

To clean marcasite, dampen a clean cloth with water and pat in baking soda. Rub this gently over the marcasites. This mixture will remove surface discolorations. Be certain to dry thoroughly with a soft cloth.

Clean rhinestones by dampening a towel with glass cleaner, rubbing the towel gently over the stones and drying with a soft cloth.

To protect both your fine antique as well as costume-jewelry collection, store it in a clean, dust-free, dry place. A jewelry case with lots of compartments is fine, but a large box is just as effective. Make sure the individual items do not roll around or touch each other in such a way that they will scratch or become entangled. Do not use plastic to wrap your jewelry because it traps moisture. Silver especially should *never* be wrapped in plastic because it causes discoloration.

## A FINAL WORD

Just what have we learned about buying antique jewelry?

First, that you begin collecting only if you have a genuine passion for the subject. Next, you fan the collector's-fever flame by research and acquisition of knowledge on the subject.

For expertise, study social and style cycles and the history and cultural patterns of the jewelry period you are interested in, and concentrate on learning about and buying jewelry from that particular era.

Learn to use the two most important tools of the jewelry-buying collector efficiently: a loupe and penlight.

Accept any gems-and-jewelry seller's romantic stories of an item's provenance with good humor, patience—and skepticism!

Find out how to correctly examine a piece of jewelry in order to detect good workmanship, maker's marks, repairs, alternations, reproductions, and condition.

Learn how to *quality rank* jewelry from the era you are most interested in; i.e., learn how to tell good, better, and best of its kind.

Recognize that while you may be able to find some outstanding antique jewelry in world markets, some of the best buys may be right in your own hometown.

Select and care for every purchase as the personal treasure it is. Realize that you may be just a temporary owner in a long line of caretakers for this lovely link to the past.

Finally, measure the joy your antique-jewelry collection brings you by the time you have invested in its acquisition, the history you have learned along the way, and the memories you are creating for the future.

# GLOSSARY

## ANTIQUE AND PERIOD JEWELRY TERMS

**Aigrette** Hair or hat ornament usually shaped like a feather or flowers on a stem. The sections are mounted on tiny springs allowing movement, which is called *en tremblant*.

**Albert** A man's vest watch chain made popular by Prince Albert of England.

**Antique** An item at least one hundred years old.

**Baguette** A gemstone cut in a rectangular cut, used mainly for small diamonds.

**Bakelite** First synthetic plastic, made from formaldehyde and phenol, invented in 1907 by Leo Hendrick Baekeland, a Belgian chemist. An important jewelry material in the 1920s and 1930s.

**Berlin iron jewelry** Cast iron jewelry, produced in Germany during the nineteenth century. Given in exchange for fine jewelry in 1813–15 to subsidize Germany's war effort.

**Bezel set** A collar of metal shaped closely over the girdle of the gemstone. Also called collet set.

**Bloomed gold** A textured finish on gold created by immersing in acid; gives a matte pitted effect.

**Bog oak** Fossilized wood from the bogs of Ireland and used for jewelry in the Victorian period.

**Bohemian garnet**  Dark red pyrope garnet.

**Bohemian glass**  Handmade glass, colored red and made in northern Czechoslovakia.

**Briolette-cut**  A teardrop-shaped cut covered with facets, used mainly in diamonds.

**Brooch**  An ornamental piece of jewelry that affixes to clothing or hats, generally with a pinback.

**Cabochon**  A stone cut and polished with a smooth, domed surface—without facets.

**Cameo**  A bas-relief carved from hardstone, shell, coral or lava.

**Cameo habillé**  A type of cameo in which the carved figure is adorned with a necklace, earrings, or diadem set with one or more small gemstones.

**Cannetille**  Open-coiled wirework technique popular in jewelry during the Georgian period and first half of the nineteenth century.

**Carat**  A unit of weight for gemstones. From 1913, one metric carat has been set as 1/5 gram, or 200 milligrams.

**Carbuncle**  In the Middle Ages, carbuncle referred to a red stone cut in cabochon form. Today it refers to garnets cut in cabochon.

**Cartouche**  Decorative ornamental tablet usually engraved with letters or symbols.

**Cast**  Jewelry-making technique of pouring molten metal into a mold to assume a shape when it cools.

**C-Clasp**  Closure for pin in the shape of a "C" and found on antique brooches and breast pins.

**Celluloid**  A plasticlike substitute for ivory. Highly flammable. Used mainly in Victorian era and early twentieth century.

**Champlevé**  Enamel decoration produced by pouring enamel into cut recesses into the surface of the metal and then firing.

**Chatelaine**  A seventeenth-century piece of jewelry for suspending seals and other useful implements (scissors, measure, etc.) from a woman's belt.

**Claw setting**  Style of setting in which the gemstone is held in place by a series of projecting claws folded down over the stone's edges, gripping it in its setting.

**Clip**  A brooch that has a hinged clip back instead of a pin-back to fasten onto clothing. Popular from 1920 to 1940.

**Cloisonné**  Enameling technique where enamel is placed into small compartments (cloisons) built onto the setting.

**Cut-steel**  Stud or rounded cut steel, faceted and set to look like a brilliant diamond. Popular from the 1760s until the late nineteenth century.

**Demantoid garnet**  A green andradite garnet called demantoid because of its adamantine luster. The green stones have an enticing sparkle and were very popular at the turn of the twentieth century. Demantoid garnets were first found in Russia in 1868.

**Demi-parure** Small ensemble of jewelry—usually brooch and earrings or a necklace and earrings.

**Doublet** Two-part assembled stone, often a garnet crown over a glass pavilion. Doublets can be made to imitate any stone.

**Die-struck/Die-stamped** Jewelry formed by pressing a softer precious metal alloy such as gold or silver into a hardened steel die.

**Dog collar** Type of necklace consisting of numerous rows of beads or pearls in a wide band worn snugly around the neck.

**Edwardian jewelry** Jewelry made during the reign of Edward VII, 1901–1910.

**Electroplating** Metal covered with a coating of another metal by using electrical current.

**Electrum** A pale yellow alloy made by mixing 20 percent gold and 80 percent silver.

**Engraving** A technique for putting design into a metal surface with incised lines using chisels or engravers.

**E.P.B.M.** Symbol used on silverplate indicating electroplated on britannia metal.

**E.P.C.** Indicates electroplating on copper.

**E.P.N.S.** Indicates electroplating on nickel silver.

**Estate jewelry** Previously owned jewelry, not necessarily antique items.

**Etruscan style** A distinctive feature of this style is granulation; i.e., minute grains of gold or silver metal soldered to a background forming a pattern.

**Faceting** The technique of cutting a gemstone into a series of planes to bring out maximum beauty and brilliance.

**Fede ring** A ring featuring two clasped hands, used as engagement ring.

**Ferronnière** A chain encircling the forehead. First worn in the sixteenth century, it was revived during the Victorian era.

**Filigree** A type of metalwork made of plain, twisted, or plaited fine metal wire.

**Findings** Those parts of jewelry that are mass-produced, such as catches, spring rings, gallery strips, pins, and clasps.

**Fine gold** Pure gold, 24 karat.

**Fob** An ornament worn with a watch and suspended by a chain—often a seal.

**Foil** A thin metal sheet, usually colored, placed in the base or in back of a setting to improve the appearance of the stone placed on top of it.

**French jet** Neither French nor jet, this term refers to black glass.

**Gemology** The study of gemstones.

**Georgian**  A term that refers to the era encompassing the reigns of kings George I, II, III, and IV (1714 to 1830).

**GIA  Gemological Institute of America.**

**Girandole**  Triple pendant earrings.

**Girdle**  The outer edge, or periphery, of a fashioned stone.

**Goldstone**  A man-made gem material cut in cabochon form for setting. The material is brown with flakes of copper, giving a spangled bronze effect.

**Gutta percha**  A hard rubber material discovered in the 1840s and used for jewelry, especially mourning jewelry.

**Hair jewelry**  Jewelry made using hair braided into various ornamental items, such as watch chains and earrings. Or jewelry that has hair in the form of thin strands, used in design.

**Hallmark**  Markings used on silver and gold in England since 1300 to designate the fineness of the metal, the town in which it was assayed, and the name of the maker. Hallmarks are also used in other European countries.

**Illusion setting**  Metal surrounding a stone making it appear to be larger than it is.

**Imitation**  A substitute for the genuine item.

**Intaglio**  Engraving or carving made below the surface of the stone material to give the impression of a design in relief.

**Intarsia**  A picture made by cutting stones in precise shapes and inlaying them flush into a background stone.

**Jabot pin**  A stickpin that impales a garment.

**Jet**  A lightweight brownish-black material; a variety of the coal family. Used in the mid–1800s for mourning jewelry.

**Lava jewelry**  Jewelry made from the lava of Mount Vesuvius popular during the Victorian era. Usually carved into cameos.

**Lavaliere**  A delicate pendant necklace worn especially during the period 1890–1910. The name is believed to be derived from the Duchess de la Vallière, mistress of Louis XIV.

**Maker's mark**  A trademark or initials stamped inside a piece to indicate the maker of the item.

**Marcasite**  Iron pyrite (fool's gold) faceted to imitate diamonds, and mounted in a pavé setting in silver or other metals. Replaced the earlier cut-steel gem imitations. Popular from the eighteenth century onward.

**Marquise**  A navette (boat-shape) cut used for diamonds and other gemstones.

**Memento mori**  Jewelry gifts given to mourners of a deceased.

**Micromosaic**  Tesserae (small bits of colored glass) placed together to form designs that appear to be painted.

**Millegrain**  A style of decoration on a setting in which a series of tiny beads (grains) of metal are raised around the edge of the setting by a knurling tool (millegrain tool). This technique was developed in the nineteenth century.

**Mourning jewelry** Jewelry worn by friends and relatives in memory of a deceased loved one.

**Muff chain** A long chain worn around the neck and passed through the muff to keep it secure to the person.

**Niello** A decorative technique that dates back to the Bronze Age; silver decorated with a dark gray metallic inlay.

**Old-European cut** A diamond cut with circular shape and large culet (small facet on pointed bottom stone); the table (large facet at top of stone) is usually small. This cutting style was commonly used between 1885 and 1915.

**Old-mine-cut** A diamond cut with a cushion shape, large culet, with the girdle placed nearly halfway between the table and culet. This cutting style was common in the last half of the nineteenth century.

**Open back** A setting that allows light to travel through a set stone.

**Parure** Suite of jewelry (usually late eighteenth to nineteenth century) that may include a necklace, pendant, brooch, earrings, and bracelets.

**Paste** Glass that has been molded, faceted, carved, or otherwise made to resemble gemstones.

*Pâte de verre* French for "glass paste." A process in which glass is ground to powder, colored, and placed in a mold before firing. This technique was used in the production of Art Nouveau jewelry.

**Pavé** Bead-set jewelry whose surface has been "paved" with small stones.

**Pavilion** The portion of the gemstone below the girdle of the stone.

**Pebble jewelry** Generally silver Scottish jewelry set with stones native to Scotland. Popular in the Victorian era.

**Pietra dura** Pieces of polished gem material set in a background of slate, lapis lazuli, or similar material.

**Pinchbeck** An alloy of copper and zinc, invented by Christopher Pinchbeck in the 1720s, which imitated gold.

**Pique** The technique of decorating tortoiseshell jewelry with inlays of gold or silver. Popular from mid-seventeenth century until twentieth century.

**Provenance** The documented history of an item, including its origin and important owners.

**Regard ring** A ring set with gemstones of which the first letter in each spells out the word REGARD. The most common stones used: Ruby, Emerald, Garnet, Amethyst, Ruby, Diamond.

**Repoussé** A decorative technique of raising a pattern on metal by punching, beating, or hammering a design from the reverse side.

**Reverse intaglio** Incised carving on the base of a rock-crystal cabochon that is then colored and backed by mother-of-pearl or similar material. Popular from late nineteenth century to first half of twentieth.

**Rhinestone** Originally a stone cut from rock crystals found in the Rhine Valley. Today, a term used to describe glass stones.

**Riviere** A gem-set necklace in which graduated stones are placed in a row in separate settings.

**Rococo** Early- to mid-eighteenth century design with curved lines, shell, scroll, and foliage motifs.

**Rose-cut** A gem-cutting style in which the stone is cut with a flat base, a pointed faceted top, and at least three regularly placed triangular facets. The style originated in India and dates from the mid-seventeenth century.

**Sautoir** A long rope of beads or chain extending below a woman's waist, sometimes terminating in a pendant or tassel.

**Seal** A carved intaglio with a design reversed so that it is readable when it is impressed in wax.

**Shank** The part of a ring which encircles the finger and to which settings are soldered.

**Shoulder** The part of the ring where the shank and the settings meet.

**Simulant** A gemstone or metal that masquerades as a precious stone or metal.

**Star setting** Popular in the late nineteenth century, this style features a stone placed in an engraved star and secured by a small grain of metal at the base of each point.

**Strass** A brilliant type of paste jewelry developed by the Parisian royal jeweler Georges Frederic Strass in 1780.

**Stomacher** An eighteenth-century jeweled ornament worn on the upper body and extending below the waistline.

**Synthetic** A man-made gemstone with the same chemical, physical, and optical properties as its natural counterpart.

**Table** The flat top facet of a gemstone.

**Torc** Sometimes spelled torque. A type of metal neck ring associated with Celtic jewelry.

**Tortoiseshell** The shell of the hawksbill turtle, it is golden yellow, with brown markings.

**Triplet** A composite stone consisting of three components that appear to be one gemstone. For example, an opal triplet consists of a thin slice of precious opal cemented to a backing of black basalt or similar material and covered with a protective cap of rock crystal.

**Vermeil** Gold that is plated on a sterling silver, bronze, or copper base.

# $\mathcal{B}$IBLIOGRAPHY

Baarsen, R. J. and Van Berge, G. *Juwelen 1820–1920*. Amsterdam: Rijksmuseum publication, 1990.

Bailey, Banks & Biddle. *Military and Naval Insignia and Novelties*. Philadelphia: Company catalog, 1916.

Bedel, Catherine. *L'Argus des Bijoux Anciens*. Paris: Pierre Belfond, 1980.

Bell, Jeanenne. *Answers to Questions About Old Jewelry (1840–1950)*. Florence, Ala.: Books Americana, Inc., 1985.

Bivins, John, Jr. and Welshimer, Paula. *Moravian Decorative Arts in North Carolina*. Winston-Salem: Old Salem, Inc., 1981.

Dorn, Sylvia O'Neill. *The Insider's Guide to Antique, Art and Collectibles*. New York: Doubleday & Company, 1974.

*The Crystal Palace Exhibition Illustrated Catalogue London 1851*. New York: Dover Publications, 1970.

Gere, Charlotte and Munn, Geoffrey C. *Artists' Jewellery*. Suffolk, England: Antique Collectors' Club, Ltd., 1989.

Haynes, Colin. *The Complete Collector's Guide to Fakes and Forgeries*. Greensboro, N.C.: Wallace-Homestead, 1988.

Hinks, Peter. *Victorian Jewelry*. New York: Portland House, 1991.

James, Duncan. *Old Jewellery*. Great Britain: Shire Publications Ltd., 1989.

Jarmin, K. W. *Military "Sweetheart" Brooches*. Suffolk: Lavenham Press Ltd., 1981.

Katcher, Philip. *American Civil War Armies Volunteer Militia*. London: Osprey Publishing, Ltd., 1989.

Kovel, Ralph and Terry. *The Kovels' Antiques & Collectibles Price List*. 16th ed. New York: Crown Publishers, Inc., 1983.

Lorene, Karen. *Buying Antique Jewelry: Skipping The Mistakes*. Seattle: Lorene Publications, 1987.

Mackay, James A. *Antiques of the Future*. New York: Universe Books, 1970.

Mason, Anita and Packer, Diane. *An Illustrated Dictionary of Jewellery*. London: Osprey Publishing, Ltd., 1973.

Matlins, Antoinette L. and Bonanno, A. C. *Jewelry & Gems, The Buying Guide*. South Woodstock, Vt: Gemstone Press, 1987.

Miller, Anna M. *Gems & Jewelry Appraising: Techniques of Professional Practice*. New York: Van Nostrand Reinhold, 1988.

———. *Illustrated Guide to Jewelry Appraising: Antique Period & Modern*. New York: Van Nostrand Reinhold, 1990.

———. *Cameos Old & New*. New York: Van Nostrand Reinhold, 1991.

Newman, Harold. *An Illustrated Dictionary of Jewelry*. London: Thames and Hudson, 1981.

Percival, MacIver. *Chats on Old Jewellery and Trinkets*. London: T. Fisher Unwin Publisher, 1912.

Ramsey, L. G. G., F. S. A., Editor. *The Complete Encyclopedia of Antiques*. New York: Hawthorn Books, 1962.

Scarisbrick, Diana and Zucker, Benjamin. *The Power of Love. Six Centuries of Diamond Betrothal Rings*. London: The Diamond Information Center, 1988.

Swaab, Shirley S. "Death as a Way of Life: Mourning Art and Customs." *Nineteenth Century*. Vol. 10, No. 2, pp. 24–29. Philadelphia: The Victorian Society, 1990.

# INDEX

Aigrette, 10. (See entremblant), 11
Art Deco, 24–27
    At-A-Glance, 25
    Bakelite jewelry, 26–27
Arts-and-Crafts, 20–21
    At-A-Glance, 20
Art Nouveau, 16–19
    American jewelers in, 18
    At-A-Glance, 19
Ashbee, Charles Robert, 20–21
Astor, Mrs. John Jacob, 3
Auction, 35–37

Baekeland, Dr. Leo, 26
Bakelite, 26–27
Beads
    cloisonne, 93
    repolishing, 93
    restringing, 92
    turquoise, 94
    value factors of, 93
Bracelets
    Bakelite, 26
    bangles, 62–67
    charms, 67
    hair, 95
    history of, 61
    mourning, 95–97
    pomander, 65
    quality of, 66–67
    Victorian reproductions, 52
    Victorian styles in, 63
Brooches
    Berlin iron, 68
    cameos in, 70

    eighteenth century, 68
    gems in, 70
    hair, 95
    history of, 67
    military, 102
    mourning, 95–97
    sweetheart, 101–102
    Victorian, 69
    Victorian motifs in, 70–71
Brunswick Blue Diamond, 153–54
Brunswick Diamond Feather Pin,
    152–53
Buttons
    converted to jewelry, 74
    in mourning jewelry, 95

Cameos, 16, 70
Carat, 40
Castellani, Fortunato Pio, 70
Cartier, Louis, 90
Cast jewelry, 109
Chains
    Albert, 75
    chatelaine, 75
    Half-Albert, 75
    history of, 75–76
    Leontine, 75
    use of, 45–46
Circa dating, 8, 9
    earrings, 81
    language of, 40
Cleaning
    amber, 164
    antique jewelry, 163–65
    coral, 164

costume jewelry, 166–67
ivory, 164
lava, 164
pearls, 165
shell, 165
tortoiseshell, 165
Collectibles, 4–6
Collections
affordable, 4
appraisals for, 147–48
building of, 143–44
insurance for, 146–47
planning, 145–46
price guides to, 149–50
Cross, 77
Cubic Zirconia, 41

Designs
Arts-and Crafts, 20–21
Art Deco, 25
Art Nouveau, 19
Edwardian, 23
Georgian, 12
Retro, 29
Victorian, 15
Designers
Art Nouveau, 18
Fabergé, 107
J. F. Backes & Co., 62
Nineteenth century, 108
Diamonds
Art Deco jewelry in, 25
cuts of, 116–17
Edwardian jewelry in, 9
Georgian jewelry in, 9
use in antique jewelry, 115–17
Die-struck jewelry, 110
Doublets, 44–45

Earrings
antique, 35
circa dating, 81–82
designs of, 79–80
girandole, 11
history of, 78
Roman, 6
screw-back, 24
Victorian, 80–81
Edwards, Charles A., 101–103
Edwardian, 21–23
At-A-Glance, 23
monarch, 21
platinum usage in, 22–23
Elements of value, 31, 54

repairs, 55
Enhanced gemstones, 41, 94

Fabergé, 53–54, 107–108
signature, 108
Fads, 105–106
Fashion, 106
Ferronniere, 106
Florentine Diamond, 154–55
Forgeries, 51

Garnets
Bohemia, 71–73
reproduction jewelry in, 73
talisman as, 73
Gemstones
agate, 114–15
amber, 114, 164
amethyst, 119–20
bloodstone, 115
carnelian, 115
coral, 115, 164
diamonds, 115, 116, 117
emeralds, 117, 118
fakes, 51
garnets, 71–73
goldstone, 118
moonstone, 118
opal, 118, 119
paste, 122–23
pearls, 119, 165
polishing, 93
ruby, 120–21
sapphire, 121
topaz, 121
uncommon to antique jewelry, 57
use in antique jewelry, 56, 114–21
use in Arts-and Crafts jewelry, 20
use in Art Nouveau jewelry, 18, 19
use in Edwardian jewelry, 23
use in Georgian jewelry, 12
use in Retro jewelry, 29
use in Victorian jewelry, 15
waxed turquoise, 94
Georgian jewelry, 9–12
At-A-Glance, 12
clues to dating, 9

Hair jewelry (See mourning
jewelry)
Dutch, 130–31
Victorian, 14
Hallmarks
assay mark, 113
early use of, 112

Russian, 113–14
sovereign's head, 113
use in gold, 112, 113
year mark, 113
*History of the World - Naturalis Historia* (Pliny the Elder), 51
House of Savoy Emerald necklace, 155–57

*Illustrated Dictionary of Jewelry* (Newman), 51, 111
Imitations, 43
misleading names in, 43–44
industrial Revolution, 7, 16, 17

Jermin, K. W., 98
Jewelry
aigrette, 10, 11
antique, 5
Arts-and-Crafts, 20–21
Art Deco, 24–27
Art Nouveau, 16–19
bracelets, 61–67
brooches, 67–71
buttons, 74
chains, 75–76
collectible, 5
counterfeit, 51
crosses, 77–78
cut-steel, 11
earrings, 78–82
Edwardian, 21–24
ferronniere, 106
forgery, 51
Georgian, 9–13
heirloom, 5
lockets/pendants, 82–83
manufacturing methods of, 109–10
married jewelry, 50
mass produced, 8
metals used in, 110–12
mourning, 14
necklaces, 84–85
new techniques in, 14
Period, 5
political pins, 103–104
reproductions, 51
Retro, 27–29
rings, 85–88
scarfpins, 88–90
Sevigne brooch, 11, 67
stickpins, 88–90
sweetheart badges, 97–103
Victorian, 13–16

Vintage, 5
watch fobs, 90–92
*Jewellery Studies* (Society of Jewelry Historian, UK), 38

Karat, 40

Lalique, Rene, 17
Lapis lazuli, 9
beads of, 93
repolishing of, 93
scarab, 9
Lieberman, Gloria, 52
Lockets/pendants
history of, 82
values, 82
Loupe, 47–49

Marcasite, 11
Markets, 124–26
antique shows, 127
auction, 35–38
European, 128–33
Married jewelry, 37, 50
Metals
cut-steel, 11
electroplating, 110
English use of, 14
German silver, 111
gold-filled, 111
hallmarks on, 112
marcasite, 11
Pinchbeck, 110
platinum, 111
sterling silver, 111
use in Arts-and Crafts, 20
use in Art Nouveau, 19
use in Early America, 111-12
use in Edwardian, 21–23
use in Georgian, 12
use in Retro, 29
use in Victorian, 15, 16
white gold, 111
Mistakes checklist, 39
Moravian jewelry, 59–60
Motifs
Arts-and-Crafts, 20–21
Art Deco, 2, 4, 25, 27
Art Nouveau, 17, 19
Edwardian, 21–24
garter, 63
Retro, 29
rose, 8
serpent, 64
Victorian, 15

Mourning jewelry
  collection of, 33
  colors of, 14
  history of, 95–97
  lockets/pendants, 82
  materials used in, 95–96
  motifs in, 14
  Victorian, 14, 95

Natural stone, 41
Necklaces
  history of, 84–85
  motifs used in, 84–85

Parure, 10
  demi-parure, 10
  Georgian, 10
Paste
  identification of, 122–23
  invented by, 122
  popularity of, 122
  use in Georgian era, 10
Penlight, 50
Period jewelry, 6
Pinchbeck, Christopher, 110
Platinum
  early use of, 111
  knife-edge setting, 23
  millegrain setting, 23
  use in Art Deco jewelry, 25
  use in Edwardian jewelry, 21–23
  use in World War II, 28
Political jewelry, 103–104
Proler, Lynette, 54, 63
Provenance, 33, 59–64

Quedlinburg Treasure, 159–62

Repairs, 55
Reproduction jewelry, 51
  Victorian, 52
  features of, 53
  values of, 53
Retro, 27–29
  At-A-Glance, 29
  materials used in, 28
Rings
  claddagh, 86
  collectibility of, 34
  fede, 86
  giardinetti, 86–87
  hair, 95
  half-hoop, 88
  history of, 85–88
  intaglio, 6
  mourning, 95

Persian, 6
posy, 86
regard, 86
Roman, 6
seal, 86
Victorian, 88
Rossetti Pocket Watch, 158–59

Scarab, 9
Scarfpins, 89–90
Sevigne brooch, 11, 67
Shopping
  alone, 138
  bargain, 139–41
  discount, 141–42
  dressing for, 136–37
  in Amsterdam, 130–32
  in London, 33, 128–29
  in Paris, 132–33
Stabilized stones, 42
Stickpins
  history of, 88
  motifs, 89
  prices of, 90
Swaab, Shirley Sue, 96–97
Sweetheart badges, 97–103
  British, 98
  Canadian, 100–101
  elements of value, 101
  Royal Artillery, 99
  types of, 99–100
Synthetic stones
  definition of, 42
  diamonds, 43
  first use of, 42
  rubies, 18
  sapphire doublets, 45
  use in Retro jewelry, 28
  value of, 43
  Verneuil, Auguste, 18

Trends, 105–107
Triplet stones, 44

Value, 54–55
Victorian, 13
  At-A-Glance, 15
  motifs, 16
  mourning jewelry, 95–97
  *Victorian Jewellery* (Flower), 81
  Victoria, Queen of England, 13

Watch fobs, 10, 90, 91, 95
Wristwatch
  cocktail, 27
  first design, 90